...A VISION OF OUR PAST

We Americans have a long-standing love affair with the trails that led our western an-
cestors toward the sunset. We have been intent on walking honestly backward in time,
starting our journey through the doors of research. What an eye opening adventure; the
photography, following the pioneers, the wild west character (sorting out the exagger-
ated truth), and compiling their treasured culinary pantry provisions. We realize we
have only portrayed a small part of the fascinating journey, along the severe trails with
harsh excitement daily, so long ago. Those pioneers were bold adventurers, willing to
take great risks. They were heeding Horace Greeley's advice, not just to "Go west, young
man" – but to "Go west young man, and grow up with the territory!" The path the pioneers followed symbolized the spirit of enterprise that nourished the American dream.
We've put together a sampling of the history exemplified-- the hopes and dreams of
all Americans for a better life. It is our hope that this book can be taken into a quiet
corner for sincere reading and enjoyment. Gabrielle's fantastic photos are her original works of art. They are incredibly poignant and moving. To me, cooking has always
been a labor of love! I've tried to put new extremely flavorful recipes in this book. You
must own our other books to have a complete collection of wholesome tasting cooking.

ROMANCING THE WEST

From The Prairie Grass To The Pantry

By Frances A. Gillette

Photography by Gabrielle Massie

Western Stories, Poems, and Quotes by
Cheri Mattson and Heidi Esteb

Typing by Brooke Tormanen

Edited and Published by Frances A. Gillette

Layout and File Preparation by
Ward Homola — Infinite Color, Inc.
www.infinitecolor.com
Gabrielle Massie — Simply Focused
www.simplyfocused.org

Print Production by WestCoast PrintShop
www.westcoastprintshop.com
Mike Williamson

ISBN# 978-0-9636066-0-0

Printed in the United States of America

Copyright © 2009 by Frances A. Gillette

First Printing

Throughout the book you'll find statements, quotes, and dialogue
taken from historical documents, postings, diaries, and other
sources. The wording was not changed or corrected.

RICH LOCAL HERITAGE

The trapping of fur-bearing animals was key to the mountain man and played a significant role in American western expansion. Meriwether Lewis recorded in his log in the winter of 1804 when wintering in Vancouver, Washington, that this plain along the river was the most habitable area west of the Mississippi River.

The most successful fur trade company was the Hudson Bay Co. in 1821 in Fort Vancouver. The fort was run by Chief Factor John McLoughlin, who would later be hailed as the Father of Oregon. It became the center of political, social, and economic interactions in the Pacific Northwest, creating a society of trappers, Native Americans and various European groups.

Local Native American tribes used nets, snares, deadfalls, clubs, etc., to obtain fur pelts. Central to the fur-trading industry was the beaver, the animal that quickly emerged as the number one prized fur. Beaver pelts became known as beaver gold. For more than 200 years this animal provided a booming business in North America and was the most valuable animal at Fort Vancouver.

"Made Beaver" was used as the unit of currency, a prime beaver skin, flesh removed, stretched and dried. The value of all trade goods was based on made beaver "plews" or pelts. The value of other furs, i.e., otter, fox, rabbit, and martin, were valued in terms of made beaver.

Captain Clark, once Lewis' superior, was let go from the army prior to their journey. This incredible fact was concealed from the men, who in turn believed Clark to be their captain.

Lewis and Clark's journey itself was admired and discussed for many years, but their actual writings, so painstakingly recorded, were not introduced for almost two hundred years.

Sacajawea, a Shoshone captive girl who is known for her help along the journey, gave birth to Jean Baptiste Charbonneau in the water. Her midwife was Lewis! Her life, rather myth-like, is definitely an intriguing part of history. Her nickname was Janey!

Jean Baptiste (Little Pomp) was a great asset to the party, as his presence provided a peaceful atmosphere for relations with the Indians. (One of Lewis and Clark's main goals was to discover and learn different Indian tribes and their customs.)

Young Baptiste was admired and loved by many. He learned four languages and grew to become an extremely proficient and sought-after guide. Perhaps his introduction to life on that incredible journey was as instrumental in the making of our history as that of his mother!

SACAJAWEA
DIED-APRIL 9, 1884
A GUIDE WITH THE
LEWIS AND CLARK
EXPEDITION
1805 ——— 1806
IDENTIFIED, 1907 BY
REV. J. ROBERTS
WHO OFFICIATED AT
HER BURIAL

ACKNOWLEDGEMENTS

First I wish to thank all who shared their prized delicious recipes, especially the following who brought their prepared recipes and props to Gabrielle for pictures: Cheryl Crume, Judy Tikka, Debbie Rinta, Merle Moore, Candy Wallace, Em Miller, Lori Homola, Heidi and Tom Esteb, Heather Uskoski, Sandra Easterly, Judy Toivonen, Richard Peldo, Shana DeRoo, Clarence and Sherry Deel, Joe Williams, Kelli Merriman, Mary and Stan Sneeden, Marv and Lark Hersey.

Thank you, our grandson Jerod Esteb for going to far distant places to capture the haunting images for this book.

Thanks a million times goes out to our granddaughter, Gabrielle Massie; without her this book would have been uncompleted. She kept the vision and the goal achievable. Oh, the pictures that girl took! Her suggestions and help have made this book what it is. We spent many beautiful hours by the campfire with her family, Joe, Trinity, and Naudia. The marshmallows after the photography were great too! Joe chose the subtitle "From The Prairie Grass To The Pantry." Excellent choice, Joe!

Much gratitude and appreciation is owed to our granddaughter, Brooke Tormanen, when I would call to tell her more typing was coming she rarely said she couldn't do it. She waited, gave up trips to the pool many times for the material and typed and typed and typed. She even took her lap top along when she went on vacation! Thanks, honey!

All of my family encouraged me. Cheri and Heidi researched and compiled several needed facts and stories. All this takes hours, and how much I appreciate their endeavors.

Dear Sandra Easterly, again, let us come to her "old west" unique home for pictures, history and shortbread. Sandra, you are special, thank you!

A big thank-you goes to Andy Devine and Jeffry Gillette for their contributions. Also, Jason Gillette and Owen Kysar for "THE FISH."

I wish everyone who will be printing or laying out a project could have the privilege of working with Mike Williamson and Ward Homola. All the way the experience has been positive. Thanks, boys!

Proof readers! The best! Janina Kerr-Bryant, Elaine Sarkinen, Paula Stepheson, Merle Moore, Heidi Esteb, Cheryl Crume, Lori Homola, Kristy Gillette, Debbie Rinta, Bethany Kadow, Heather Uskoski, and Brooke Tormanen, you deserve so many sincere thank-yous!

Thanks to all who have purchased my past books. A huge thank-you, to Len, Janet, Darci, and Christa Williams at the local Amboy Market. They have sold hundreds of my books. I went to school with Len and Janet. He provides all of North Clark County with boxes and boxes of fresh produce!

"Eastward I go by force; but westward I go free...."
– Henry David Thoreau

LAND!

The unbridled promise for a new life! Millions marched toward the same horizon....with a spirit of enterprise and adventure. To go west was instinct...deeply planted in the human soul. Perhaps this explains why people were so willing to sacrifice so much, and take the great risks required on the journey. Thank God for all things!

SPICED HASH BROWNS

A really good breakfast treat!

3-5 large potatoes, peeled
½ dozen green onions, chopped
⅓ cup jalapeno peppers, finely diced
1 tablespoon flour

1 teaspoon salt
½ teaspoon pepper
1 beaten egg

Shred potatoes and soak in cold water for a couple minutes. Drain potatoes, rinsing off the starch. Add onions and peppers. Mix flour, salt and pepper; sprinkle over potatoes and toss to mix. Stir egg into potatoes. Drop by large spoonfuls of potato mixture onto a hot greased skillet. Cover and cook until browned and golden, about 10 minutes on medium heat. Turn and cook until potatoes are browned and done. Makes 4 servings.

WORKING MAN CHEESE PANCAKES

Heidi's kids brought many friends home to stay weekends; she made sure they came back by serving real big breakfasts. These beloved pancakes were the most requested served with backstrap. Incredibly easy but undeniably special!

Good batter of your choice
Good cheese of your choice
Real butter
Mrs. Buttersworth's syrup
Home canned peaches (optional)

Have skillet piping hot; add 1-2 tablespoons oil to batter. Pour in 4-5 inch rounds. Place slice of cheese on top. Turn when bubbles in batter appear. Fry cheese side down for 2-3 minutes. Flip on large platter; serve with butter and syrup. Tom likes peaches to crown the top.

SWEET BREAKFAST FRENCH TOAST

Oven baked with fruit sauce. Wonderful to serve when you have overnight company.

1 loaf white bread, ends discarded
⅓ cup sugar, plus extra for sprinkling
1 teaspoon cinnamon
½ teaspoon baking powder
6 large eggs
2 teaspoons vanilla
2 cups milk

While French toast is baking, thicken your favorite fruit for topping. You can also use fruit pie filling from a can. Heat oven to 375°. Butter a 9x13 baking dish. Arrange enough bread slices in a single layer to cover the bottom of the baking dish. Cut remaining slices in half, arranging them in overlapping rows on top of first layer. There should be 3 rows of bread, ½ slices on top of full slices. Set aside. Beat together sugar, cinnamon, baking powder, eggs, and vanilla until well blended. Gradually mix in milk. Slowly pour egg mixture over bread; let soak for 5 minutes. Bake 30-40 minutes or until French toast is puffed. Sprinkle top of French toast with sugar; broil until sugar is melted and French toast is browned. When French toast is browned, top with thickened fruit and serve immediately.

OUT ON THE RANGE

BOILED COFFEE

FOR ANY COWBOY

Use 1 heaping tablespoon medium-ground coffee for each cup cold water. Pour in water and bring slowly to a boil, stirring coffee down occasionally. Remove from fire immediately and let stand in a warm place 3-5 minutes. Pour ¼ cup cold water into pot to settle grounds. Coffee will be slightly cloudy.

Water was so scarce in some parts, if folks had potatoes for a meal, they washed the potatoes first, their feet next, then made coffee with the water left. Mighty good strong coffee!   —Old Timer

Though coffee has been known to mankind since the Middle Ages, it was a luxury in frontier America. Sometimes the pioneer mother made hot, coffee-like drinks of dried wheat, barley, or certain roots, roasted and ground. In the South, sweet potatoes were sliced thin, browned in the oven, broken into bits, and ground in a coffee mill. Grandparents talk about drinking "sweet potato coffee" during and after the Civil War period. But when did coffee become popular in Colonial America? When England taxed the tea being imported to America, the colonists refused to buy it and pay the tax (which resulted in the Boston Tea Party), causing them to look for an alternative hot drink.

COFFEE MISCELLANY

- The coffee tree yields an average of one pound of coffee per year.
- To make a roasted pound of coffee it takes approximately 4000 beans.
- All coffee trees are grown within 1000 miles of the equator.

OLD FASHIONED OATMEAL CEREAL

This cereal is a great way to start your day.
Use toppings of your choice for a delicious breakfast.

1 cup old fashioned oats

½ teaspoon salt

2 cups water

Boil water with salt. Stir in oats. Cook 5-10 minutes to the consistency you like, stirring occasionally. Top with cream or butter and brown sugar. Enjoy!

ENRICHED FARINA MUSH

Full of iron and so good for breakfast!

2 cups milk

½ teaspoon salt

⅓ cup Farina

Bring milk just to a boil. Add salt. Gradually add Farina, stirring constantly with a wire whisk until blended. Reduce heat to low; simmer, uncovered 2-3 minutes or until thickened, stirring frequently. Dish up into bowls and enjoy with butter, cream or milk. Raisins, brown sugar, or dates are excellent on this cereal.

HASTY PUDDING

A wonderful recipe for breakfast.

1 teaspoon salt
1 cup yellow cornmeal
4 cups water

In a bowl combine cornmeal and 1 cup
cold water. In a kettle bring 3 cups water and 1
teaspoon salt to boiling. Carefully
stir in cornmeal mixture, making sure it does not
lump. Cook over low heat, stirring occasionally
for 10-15 minutes.
Serve cereal with butter, brown sugar,
and cream. Makes 6 servings.

WESTERN OMELET

What a great way to get in protein and veggies to start the busy day!

6 eggs
½ cup sour cream
½ teaspoon salt
½ teaspoon pepper
½ cup cooked crumbled sausage
   or chopped cooked bacon
⅓ cup onion, chopped
1 cup sliced mushrooms
1 cup grated potatoes
1 cup grated cheese, your choice
2 tablespoons each, butter and olive oil

Beat eggs; add sour cream, salt and pepper. Mix well. Cook in a skillet, onions, mushrooms, meat and potato in oil until onions are tender and mixture is lightly browned. Pour egg mixture over all; make sure eggs go under meat, onions and potatoes. Cook slowly on low heat with lid on skillet until eggs are set, about 8 minutes.
Sprinkle with cheese.

PUMPKIN BREAD

2 ½ cups white flour
1 cup whole wheat flour
2 teaspoons baking soda
1 ½ teaspoons salt
1 teaspoon cinnamon
1 cup white sugar
1 cup brown sugar
1 cup butter, melted
3 eggs
1 cup buttermilk
2 cups pumpkin, mashed
1 cup pecans, chopped
1 cup raisins

Combine all dry ingredients in a bowl.
Add the rest of the ingredients. Mix until
smooth. Pour into greased pans. For
small pans, bake 40 minutes. Bake larger
pans for 50-60 minutes. Bake at 350˚. Cool.
Slice and serve with butter or cream cheese.

Coffee

Fragrant, sparkling, amber-clear coffee is truly a drink of a thousand delights! Rare bouquet...pungent flavor...mellow smoothness...........all in one glorious beverage. Small wonder that the secrets of making the perfect cup of coffee are so coveted and well worth knowing!

A cup of excellent coffee may be made by any one of several methods: percolated, drip, steeped or boiled. We can't forget French pressed.

America will never be destroyed from the outside. If we falter and lose our freedoms, it will be because we destroyed ourselves.

Abraham Lincoln

OVERNIGHT BUCKWHEAT FLAPJACKS

Aunt Margaret and Uncle Paul made these old-fashioned buckwheat pancakes when I was a young lass. These delicious flapjacks will bring you back in time.

2 ½ cups flour

1 cup buckwheat flour

1 teaspoon salt

1 tablespoon yeast

¾ teaspoon baking soda

2 cups warm water

3 tablespoons brown sugar

2 tablespoons melted butter

Combine flours and salt in a large bowl. Soften yeast in warm water; stir in 1 tablespoon of brown sugar. After yeast is dissolved, pour this mixture into large bowl with flour. Mix well. Cover bowl and leave on counter overnight. In the morning, stir batter and add the rest of the brown sugar, soda, and melted butter. Mix; cook on greased griddle.

TREES

Trappers...traders...explorers...all three
Traveled West by land and sea
Wrote in their journals and diaries and more –
Letters and learnings and memories galore!
In writing their findings, few failed to mention
Of the great dense forests that grew trees with dimension
From the Redwoods, Fir and the Evergreen,
Tall Pine and Spruce like they'd never seen!
Upon viewing this majesty – from the Rockies to the Pacific –
Their report to the East was precise and specific:
"Always see the forest for the trees – it's a Must!
And hang a sign on your wagon – GO WEST OR BUST!"

APPLE COFFEE CAKE

After tasting the delightful coffee cake at the Monticello Antique Mall, I decided to make it in my own kitchen, the cake turned out fantastic.

1 cup butter, softened

2 cups sugar

3 eggs

1 cup sour cream

1 teaspoon almond extract

3 cups flour

½ teaspoon salt

1 teaspoon baking powder

¼ teaspoon baking soda

Cream together the first five ingredients; add dry ingredients and beat with a hand mixer about two minutes. Grease a 9x13 pan. Put one half of the dough in the pan and spread out evenly. Next put a layer of the thickened apples listed below. Now drop spoonfuls of dough on top of apples. Spread evenly. Bake at 325° 45-50 minutes. Frost and sprinkle with almonds.

THICKENED APPL

Boil 4 cups sliced apples starting to get tender. ½ cup brown sugar an teaspoon cinnamon. M tablespoons cornstarch little water and add to a Boil. Remove from heat.

FROSTING

1 cup powdered sugar

2 tablespoons melted butter

1 teaspoon almond extract

½ teaspoon milk

SOURDOUGH BREAD

Once you get the sourdough starter good and sour you can attempt this good bread recipe. Sourdough making is an art, so good when done right! You can add 1 tablespoon of yeast that has been dissolved in ¼ cup water and a little more flour – bread actually tastes the same. (Remember that bread can be made without the added yeast.)

2 cups sourdough starter

4 cups flour, more if needed

2 tablespoons sugar

1 teaspoon salt

2 tablespoons butter, softened

Mix dry ingredients into a bowl, making a well in the center. Pour sourdough starter and dissolved yeast into well. Add enough flour to make a soft dough for kneading. Knead in butter on floured board for 10-12 minutes. Place in a greased round pan. Cover and let rise until doubled in size. Bake at 375° for about 1 hour. Makes 1 loaf. Recipe can be doubled.

SOURDOUGH STARTER

For years I had a sourdough starter to make bread and pancakes. Paula Stephenson gave me the starter handed down to her from her mother-in-law, Selma Stephenson.

Dissolve 1 package dry yeast in ½ cup warm water. Sprinkle with 1 tablespoon sugar. When dissolved, add 2 cups warm water (potato water is excellent) and 2 cups flour. Beat until smooth. Cover with a cloth. Let stand at room temperature 5 to 10 days, or until bubbly; stir 2-3 times each day. To store, transfer sourdough starter to a jar and cover with cheese cloth. Refrigerate. To use starter, bring desired amount to room temperature. To replenish starter after using, stir ¾ cup flour, ¾ cup water, and 1 teaspoon sugar into remaining amount. Cover; let stand at room temperature at least one day or until bubbly. Refrigerate for later use.

WILD BILL HICKOCK

Handsome as the devil, ye say? O, yes! Standing 6 ft. tall, with dancing eyes and curling hair. Decked to the nines...here comes James B. Hickock..."Wild Bill"! Serving our country to make it stand as tall as he, Wild Bill's claims to fame were many. A marksman, constable, teamster, federal scout and guerilla fighter he was. A marshal in several towns and a gambler in several bars. Hickock drew a crowd! But alas, as life would have it, ol' Bill fell in love, and like in stories told through the ages, a heartache occurred. In the tussle of gunfight, Hickock's quarrel over his girl came to a head as he faced his competition. They stood eight feet apart, and both drew their guns. Wild Bill stood standing, the other guy was done. But in the silent shadows stood another man. Hickock fired two shots and realized too late it was his friend! Another marshal. No longer was Bill required to give his skill and gift of guns to the U.S. This man, who wore two pistols even as he slept, gave up this life to touring the country with "Buffalo Bill." While gambling one night, Hickock was shot in the back of the head by a stranger whose only motive was to kill a famous gunman. And a famous gunman this stranger did kill! May we remember Wild Bill Hickock and the trails he blazed for our country!

SIDE PORK

We love this delicious pork fried crisp and crunchy. Complements a pancake breakfast.

Place pork (looks like bacon) in ½ cornflake crumbs and ½ flour. Salt and pepper and coat both sides with crumbs and flour. Fry until crisp. Drain on paper towels.

SWEET PEPPERED BACON

Everyone wants this recipe! Fix it for company soon.

Fry bacon until done. Drain grease. Turn down stove top to low. Sprinkle with pepper and brown sugar. Heat until sugar is melted into bacon. Serve.

BREAKFAST PIZZA

Little children love this nutritious breakfast pizza. You only need ½ hour and pizza will be ready to eat. Play around with what you have in the refrigerator.

1 cup thinly-sliced ham, crumbled bacon
   or sausage
1 cup grated Swiss cheese
½ cup sliced mushrooms
3 green onions, sliced

Butter
4 eggs, beaten
¾ cup half and half
½ teaspoon salt
¼ teaspoon pepper

Roll out pie crust to fit 12-inch pizza pan. Pat dough into pan. Bake at 400° for 7 minutes on lowest rack in oven. Place ham or sausage and cheese over crust. Sauté onions and mushrooms in butter, then pour over meat and cheese. Pour beaten eggs, half and half, and seasoning over top. Bake at 400° for approximately 20 minutes until set. Slice and serve with sour cream.

PIZZA CRUST

1 ½ cups flour
⅔ cup butter
½ teaspoon salt
3-4 tablespoons water

Mix flour, salt, and butter. Cut in until dough resembles small crumbs. Add cold water, mixing with fork until moistened.

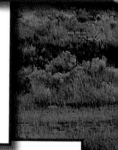

LUMBERJACK PRUNE SAUCE

Those loggers of the Northwest loved this spiced sauce on their breakfast pancakes.

1 ½ cups water

1 cup dried prunes, chopped

¼ teaspoon cinnamon

⅛ teaspoon cloves

⅛ teaspoon allspice

2 tablespoons brown sugar

Bring all ingredients to a boil. Let simmer for 15 minutes. Serve warm.

CORNMEAL PANCAKES

We like these Western pancakes for a change. Try them.

1 ½ cups flour

½ cup cornmeal

2 tablespoons sugar

1 teaspoon baking soda

1 teaspoon salt

2 cups buttermilk

2 eggs, beaten

3 tablespoons butter, melted

Sift together dry ingredients. Add buttermilk, eggs and butter. Stir just until dry ingredients are moistened. Fry on lightly greased griddle.

HOMEMADE SAUSAGE

Cowboys like their sausage spicy and full of sage. This is a very good recipe; you can add garlic, cayenne pepper or whatever.

8 pounds ground pork

4 tablespoons salt

4 teaspoons black pepper

1 ½ teaspoons ground cloves

3 teaspoons ground red pepper

5 teaspoons ground sage

Mix the seasonings and work them thoroughly into the sausage. You can freeze the sausage as is or it can be stuffed into natural casings.

CORN, America's most important native food plays a recurring role in history. First cultivated by the Indians, it sustained waves of pioneers and nation builders. Now it feeds the world.

Three Forks of the Missouri
April 21, 1810

Mr. Pierre Chouteau, Esq.
DEAR SIR and BROTHER-IN-LAW:- I had hoped to be able to write you more favorably than I am now able to do. The outlook before us was much more flattering ten days ago than it is today. A party of our hunters was defeated by the Blackfeet on the 12th. There were two men killed, all their beaver stolen, many of their traps lost, and the ammunition of several of them, and also seven of our horses. We set out in pursuit of the Indians but unfortunately could not overtake them. We have recovered forty-four traps and three horses, which we brought back here, and we hope to find a few more traps.

CHIEF JOSEPH

Nez Perce (1840-1904)

Known as Hin-mah-too-yah-lat-kekt

(Thunder Coming Up Over Land From Water)

Chief Joseph of the Nez Perce tribe of the Wallowa Valley in N.W. Oregon, was known for his persistent resistance to the U.S. Government's attempts to force his tribe onto reservations. In 1877, he refused one last time and tried to lead 800 of his people to Canada. All along the 1500 mile journey through Idaho and Montana, they valiantly fought the U.S. Army. Just 40 miles from Canada, they were trapped. Cold, hungry, and desperate, the remaining 431 Nez Perce gave up. They were beaten; defeat lay as a damp wool blanket upon their backs. On October 5th, 1877, Chief Joseph made his speech of surrender: "I am tired of fighting. Our chiefs are killed. Looking Glass is dead. Toohulhulsote is dead. The old men are all dead. It is the young men who say yes or no. He who led the young men is dead. It is cold and we have no blankets. The little children are freezing to death. My people, some of them, have run away to the hills and have no blankets, no food. No one knows where they are – perhaps freezing to death. I want to have time to look for my children and see how many I can find. Maybe I shall find them among the dead. Hear me, my chiefs. I am tired. My heart is sick and sad. From where the sun now stands, I will fight no more forever."

PLANKED SALMON

This you must try. It is also a good way to cook steelhead and trout. Hey, don't think it looks too hard, it is well worth your time. Very fun!

Choose 2 thick cedar boards, or any non-resinous boards or planks. Soak in water 2-3 hours. Build a fire with rocks around to reflect heat towards fish. Allow the fire to burn down to coals inside the rocks. Place the filleted fish skin side down onto boards. Brush with melted butter, sprinkle with brown sugar, squeeze one lemon over fish. Sprinkle cracked pepper and salt over all. Cover ends of boards with foil to catch drippings. Rotate planks to ensure even cooking. Cook until fish flakes in the thickest part. You may have to attach fish with nails and stand planks upward for part of cooking.

BROCCOLI CORN BREAD

A wonderful easy recipe from Mary Sneeden.

1 (16 oz.) package frozen broccoli, thawed
1 cup cottage cheese
5 eggs
1 box Jiffy Muffin Mix
1 stick butter
1 onion, chopped
½ teaspoon salt

Sauté chopped onion in butter. Mix all ingredients together with onion. Put mixture in greased 9x13 or 8x8 inch pan and bake at 350° for 45 minutes. When lightly browned, remove from oven and enjoy plain or with butter.

**WHEN THE GOING GETS TOUGH
THE TOUGH GET GOING!**

HEARTY STEEL CUT OAT CEREAL

*A favorite at our house. We would fix it more often if it didn't
take 20 minutes to cook. One feels fulfilled with this good
cereal in your belly for any meal of the day. A rustic texture
that is all at once rich, hearty, and healthy!*

Toast oats and nuts in a 400° oven, about 5
minutes. Oats and nuts can be stored.

3 cups water

½ teaspoon salt

1 cup pecans, chopped

1 cup steel cut oats

Bring oats and nuts to a boil in salted water. Reduce heat; cover
and cook 20 minutes, stirring occasionally. Remove from heat and
serve with butter, brown sugar, and/or half and half. Raisins,
dried cranberries or fresh fruit are also good on the cereal.

BARE BACK TRAIL MIX

A wonderful treat for hunting, camping, or just
to have in a jar at home. Recipe from our daughter, Heather.

Granola

Combine together:

2 cups old-fashioned oats

2 tablespoons maple syrup

2 tablespoons honey

Bake in a shallow pan at 375° for about 10 minutes;
Stir once. Pour mixture in large bowl.
Roast in the same shallow pan:

2 cups pecans

2 cups walnuts

1 cup almonds

Bake at 375° for 10 minutes. Add to granola in
bowl. Cool. Add and stir into granola nut mixture:

1 cup peanuts

1 cup raisins

2 Hershey chocolate candy bars, cut up

Mix all together and enjoy.

 GOLD

Nothing in American history outshines the gold rush days. Amazing accounts and adventures have been told, and still today hold rapt fascination. Man's quest for treasure is a burning desire beginning with time, so when the ground glittered before their eyes, these poor miners were literally star struck. Something close to insanity shook the earth as decent, hard working family men dropped anything they were holding or working on in the middle of the day and ran off to California. In this excitement, the radical growth spurt taking place escalated San Francisco's population from 429 to 25,000 overnight. Men asked themselves if they were going mad. The destiny of the West changed drastically from this fairy-tale-come-true phenomenon. Money was made in unheard-of proportions; many miners made $1,000 dollars a day. One man made $9,000 in 24 hours. $400 million came out of the Comstock Lode. The fever was at a high pitch. This catalyst changed relations with the Indians for the worse, as white men flocked in droves demanding more land. As a result, the wagon trains which had lumbered along on fairly friendly terms with the Indians were viciously attacked. The ironies of life dictate that we must sacrifice one thing as we gain another, and all that glitters is not gold.

COWBOY EGGS AND SPUDS

This recipe reminds me of our dear friend, Ward Stephenson. He served us the best spuds and bacon when we lived across the road from him and Paula. He could cook!

6 slices bacon

5 cups hash browns

½ cup green onions, chopped

4 eggs

3 tablespoons parmesan cheese, grated

In your largest skillet, cook bacon until crisp. Remove, crumble, and set aside. Spread potatoes evenly in grease and salt and pepper them. Add chopped green onion and seasoning of choice. Cook until spuds are done. Push potatoes to the edge of the skillet. Drop eggs into the center of the pan; cover skillet for a couple minutes. Remove cover and add crumbled bacon and grated cheese on top. Replace cover until eggs are done. Serve.

MADE TO MEASURE

How fortunate we are to have measuring cups from our mothers and grandmothers. Also, we can find them at flea markets, antique stores, and garage sales. These graceful servants of the kitchen are worthy of display. Much of what makes a measuring cup so charming is that it was designed to be used.

COLORFUL KITCHEN COLLECTIBLES

Utensils with brightly painted wooden handles brought color and cheer to the all white kitchens of the 1920's and '30s. You can find them now in your grandma's kitchen drawers or at antique shops.

SWEET APPLE CINNAMON BISCUITS

With the first fresh apples of the season, your family will line up just from the smell to taste these very good cinnamon roll biscuits. So tender and delicious with cream.

2 cups flour

1 tablespoon baking powder

1 teaspoon salt

¼ teaspoon baking soda

¼ cup vegetable oil or melted butter

¾ cup buttermilk

¾ cup brown sugar

1 teaspoon cinnamon

2 cups grated apple

½ cup butter, melted, plus ½ cup butter, softened

Combine flour, baking powder, salt, and baking soda in a bowl, mix well. Stir in melted butter/oil. Add buttermilk and stir until blended. Knead dough on a lightly floured board, about 10 times. Roll dough into a 15x8 inch rectangle. Pre-heat oven to 400˚. Grease a cast iron skillet or 9 inch round baking pan. Sprinkle with brown sugar. Use about ½ cup butter, softened, to spread on dough. Sprinkle with sugar and cinnamon. Spread grated apples on top. Roll up rectangle, jelly roll fashion, starting from one long side. Pinch seam to seal. Cut the rolls into ½ inch slices; place cut side up, in prepared skillet or baking pan. Bake until slightly browned, about 20 minutes. Serve warm with cream.

MOMMY'S BAKED BEANS

Recipe from Shana DeRoo. Her Mother passed away in 2000 and Shana tells us how much she misses this "sure-hit" yummy bean dish that her "mommy" made. Shana stole the recipe from her private files.

1 7-lb can Van De Camp's Pork and Beans

1 large onion, chopped

4 tablespoons fresh minced garlic

1 pound chopped bacon or bacon ends

2 cups brown sugar

1 cup molasses

1 cup yellow mustard

1 cup Heinz Ketchup

2 tablespoons garlic powder

1 tablespoon Wright's Hickory Smoke
   seasoning liquid

Mix all ingredients in a roasting pan. If you prefer sweeter beans add more sugar. If you prefer stronger smoke seasoning, add more. If a tangier taste is preferred, add more mustard. Taste-test before baking. Bake at 375 uncovered for 90 minutes, stirring occasionally. Remove from oven and allow to cool.

O LORD WILL I MAKE IT?

O how will I finish this trek before me?
I know that I dare not look too far behind,
My past is but wisdom's bible, while my future
Lies in the wagon wheel's continual grind.
Thick, silent dust blinds my reality, while
Hard loneliness crusts over my heart.
O Lord will I make it?
From everything I love I've had to depart!

My baby lies still; a shattered memory
Forever buried on this endless way.
My dear husband, he pushes forward,
From this burning focus, he cannot stray:
"a better place" he tells me
"to freedom, to land, to more!"
Oh Lord, will I make it?
I'm depleted to my core.

I wearily shuck one more "treasure"
Accommodating for this wagon's small space.
I try to convince myself it all means nothing
They are merely "things" I can replace
I'm a helpless pilgrim, traveling through foreign land
Please hear my prayer as I give myself to you.
Oh Lord will I make it?
Will you please carry me through?

–From the diary of a lonesome traveler

From the Missouri River to California, the trek on the Oregon Trail was about twenty-two hundred miles.

The fixed routine on the wagon trail began with a 7 o'clock bugle call for breakfast. The wagon train moved in a single file; the "nooning period" divided the day. A meal, then rest, then the afternoon trek began, continuing until dusk. Wagons formed a circle at night, with a campfire, meal, and songs to end the day. Fourteen miles a day was the average distance traveled, with about 5 months totaling the time taken for the completion of the 2000 mile journey.

People and children as young as 13 walked the grueling journey from behind the wagon, to watch that nothing or no one fell behind. At nightfall, after trekking 15 long miles, the pioneers had dust packed so thickly inside their eyes, ears, and noses they could scarcely breathe. Often times the lack of water made it impossible to bathe. Morning came early, only to begin another dusty day!

OLD-FASHIONED APPLESAUCE

We call it chunky applesauce and it is our favorite using Transparent or Gravenstein apples. I freeze this good sauce in pints for winter time.

Wash and quarter the amount of apples desired for applesauce. Core apples and peel each quarter. Place apple quarters into a heavy kettle. Add 1 to 3 inches of water, depending on the juiciness of the apples used. Simmer until tender and apple pieces are falling apart. Sweeten to taste (about ¼ cup sugar to 5 apples); bring to a boil. Pour into bowl. Cool. Sprinkle with cinnamon.

YUMMY RHUBARB SAUCE

So good in early spring. You will plant your own rhubarb once you taste this sauce!

Wash and cut rhubarb into small 1 inch pieces. Follow recipe for applesauce except omit cinnamon and add much more sugar.

"It was a hard land, and it bred hard men to hard ways." – Louis L'Amour

FRIED ZUCCHINI

We love the first small zucchini from our garden. Peel and cut zucchini into thin slices with the skin left on. Dip zucchini into egg and milk (1 egg to 2 tablespoons milk), then into finely crushed cracker crumbs. Fry in hot grease (I use olive oil and butter) until both sides are crisp and brown. Salt and pepper to taste.

BBQ TRI-TIP

A winner from Joseph M. Williams. Very delicious blend of flavors, bringing out memorable flavors in the beef. Joe says "For patient beef lovers, perfect for social get-togethers as you are able to visit over the cooking." Fire up the BBQ!

Prepare sauce before tri-tip is placed on BBQ.
French's yellow mustard

DRY RUB SPREAD

1 tablespoon paprika	1 tablespoon cumin
¼ cup brown sugar	1 teaspoon salt
¼ cup chili powder	1 teaspoon black pepper

DIPPING SAUCE
Good on any BBQ.

½ cup onion, diced	½ cup pineapple, chopped, with juice
¼ cup minced garlic	1 tablespoon cayenne pepper
½ cup white sugar	⅛ teaspoon olive oil
¼ cup brown sugar	Kraft Hickory Smoked BBQ sauce

Add oil to fry pan; brown onion and garlic. Mix in bottle of Kraft sauce and rest of ingredients. Stir to a boil. Place meat on foil. Apply French's yellow mustard generously over meat. Cover entire meat with dry rub over mustard. Fold foil around meat, making a bowl. Drop 4-6 spoonfuls of sauce on top of meat. Cover top with 2nd foil. Cover completely with 3rd foil. Cook 1 hour to 1 ½ hours depending on size of meat, with BBQ heat about medium temperature. Flip meat over 3-4 times during cooking. Remove meat from foil; save juice. Place meat directly on grill, flip 1-3 times, pouring excess juice on meat. After meat is done, remove and serve with dipping sauce. Allow meat to set 5-10 minutes before cutting into it. A treat!

CORN MEAL BUNS

This good recipe is from Ima Massie.
She got it from Cleo Williamson years ago.

In a heavy pan heat:

4 cups milk

1 cup butter

⅔ cup yellow cornmeal

1 cup sugar

1 teaspoon salt

Boil for a few minutes. Cool.

Add:

4 beaten eggs

3 tablespoons yeast dissolved in ½ cup warm water.

Add:

8 cups flour

Mix and let it rise. Punch down and let rise again. Roll out to ½ inch thick, cut out buns, place on pan. Let rise again. Bake at 400° for about 15 minutes or until buns are golden. Ima tells us that the boiled mixture can also be served as hot cereal. She reports serving it to her large family throughout their young life at home; now they all want the recipe to serve their children. For cereal cut back on the butter and sugar.

.....THE WEST WAS OPENED UP...

"Never in this land before us and never here after us will a land know such a people as a man we call the cowboy ..... his hat, his bandana, his unique brand of lingo, all his devil deeds of daring, bold and skillful in the saddle, brave ridin' in the rambling ..... wild and eager while exploring in a land that calls him with a challenge." – Johnny Cash

NO KNEAD BREAD

We were invited to Bob and Rachel Rose's for supper. She served this very delicious bread and told us: "You can use whatever type of flour you like in this recipe — I buy whole wheat, rye, and gluten flour in bulk at Winco. Bake both loaves at the same time if you have two large pots with lids that will fit in your oven."

8 cups white unbleached flour and more
    for shaping
2 ⅔ cups whole wheat flour
1 cup rye flour
¾ cup gluten flour, you can use regular flour
1 teaspoon instant yeast (rapid rise)
7 teaspoons salt
6 ½ cups warm water

Combine all dry ingredients in a large bowl, then add 6 ½ cups warm water, mix again; cover with plastic wrap or Tupperware lid. Let sit 12-18 hours at 70° or so, or until dough is dotted with bubbles. If you like a sourdough taste, let it rise 18 hours. It will be ready sooner in warm weather. Turn out on floured counter top; sprinkle with more flour. Fold over once or twice. Cover with plastic wrap and let rest 15 minutes. Using just enough flour to keep from sticking, shape dough into 2 balls. Dust a cotton (not terry) towel with flour, wheat bran or cornmeal. Put dough on towel and dust with more of same. Cover with towel and let rise 2 or 3 hours. 30 minutes before dough is ready, preheat oven to 450°. Put heavy covered pot (cast iron, enamel, ceramic or Pyrex, about 6 quart) in oven to heat. Carefully remove pot from oven. Put one dough ball in pot, shake a little, cover and bake 30 minutes. Remove lid and bake another 12-30 minutes until browned. Cool on rack. Repeat for second loaf. Do not grease or spray pot before adding dough. The bread will come out very easily. Be sure to let a ceramic pot cool before washing it out.

The old-time bunkhouse cooks or trail cooks came in all ages and sizes. They were kings of their own domain and their domain was within 100 yards of where they cooked. The trail foreman or boss usually did not tell them what to do; they were their own bosses. And you'd best not complain about what they cooked! The cook also dubbed as a barber and a doctor. One of their favorite remedies for colds was: Mix ¼ oz. gum camphor in ½ teaspoon goose oil; put on a flannel cloth around your neck and on the chest. Also rub some on the nose.

> There are two things we own. Our name while we live, and ability to know pain and suffering.
> —CRAZY HORSE

APPLE CIDER STEW

So yummy and tangy! From Maria Tormanen.

2 pounds stew meat

1 bouillon cube

Pepper and salt

2 tablespoons apple cider vinegar

3 tablespoons oil

1 apple, diced

1 cup onion, diced

3 potatoes, diced

1 piece celery, diced

4 carrots, diced

3 tablespoons flour

water

¼ teaspoon ground thyme

salt

2 cups apple cider

Salt and pepper stew meat liberally. Heat 1 tablespoon oil on medium high. Fry 1 pound of meat at a time, 3 minutes or so per side. Add 1 tablespoon oil; fry remaining meat. Add 1 tablespoon oil; fry onion and celery until soft. Add flour and thyme; cook for 1 minute. Pour in cider and scrape all brown bits off bottom of pan. Add vinegar and bouillon cube; cook 1 hour and simmer. Do not boil. Add apple, potatoes, carrots, and desired amount of water. Simmer till meat is tender and potatoes are done. Salt if needed.

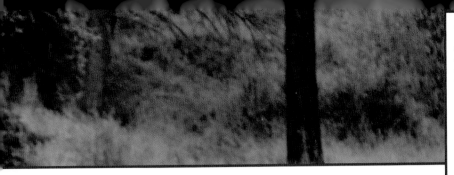

INDIAN CORN STICKS

Memorable from childhood days. Mother made these cornmeal treats in the corn stick cast iron pans.

1 cup cornmeal
½ cup flour
½ teaspoon salt
1 cup milk
1 egg
2 tablespoons lard, melted

Mix cornmeal, flour, and salt; add milk, egg and lard. Beat until smooth. Fill well-greased corn stick pans almost to the top. Bake at 425° for about 15 minutes. Serve hot sticks with butter and molasses.

INDIAN FRY BREAD

retend you are out in the hills, long ago.

1 package yeast
1 ½ cups warm water
2 tablespoons sugar
3 cups flour, maybe a little more

1 teaspoon baking powder
½ teaspoon salt
Vegetable oil

n mixing bowl, dissolve yeast and sugar in warm water. Stir in flour, salt and baking owder. Knead one minute. Cover. Let rise for ½ hour. Pat bread out to ½ inch thickness; cut n wedges. Heat oil (1 ½ inches) in a large skillet. Fry wedges until golden brown. Serve vith butter and honey.

JESSE JAMES

Have you ever really stopped and thought about the tremendous aftershock the Civil War caused? We can understand that it was a tragic situation, maybe even a necessary evil, in the creation of our country and its freedoms. But when the war was over, and "Johnny came marching home" a hero, once again, where did the lonesome drifters end up? War and its atrocities never ended for some of the Confederate Guerilla Soldiers like Jesse James. With the shame of having lost the war to the no-good blue-coats, it was easy to saddle up, ride out, and do harm to anything Republican. Jesse was no exception. He, along with his brother, Frank, The Younger Gang, and a bunch of other staunch hearts, cut a swath through banks, trains, stagecoaches, and steamboats. These outlaws shot countless guns, sometimes for no reason, acquiring an almost heroic reputation. They banked a total of nearly half a million dollars, and killed at least 21 men. The Youngers were captured and sent to prison for life, while Jesse and Frank continued robbing banks. Finally, Robert Ford, a former James gang member, shot Jesse, age 35, in the back, killing him. Frank James shifted gears, lecturing on tour about the evils of crime. He lived to a ripe old age, his income only a $1.50 a day from tourists coming to gawk at the paraphernalia from his past. Frank James denied accusations about his exploits till his dying day, stating it had never been as bad as the public would want to believe. Now who was that man that claimed "only the good die young"?

REWARD!
- DEAD OR ALIVE -

$5,000.$^{.00}_{x x}$ will be paid for the capture of the men who robbed the bank at

NORTHFIELD, MINN.

They are believed to be Jesse James and his Band, or the Youngers.

All officers are warned to use precaution in making arrest. These are the most desperate men in America.

Take no chances! Shoot to kill!!

J. H. McDonald,
SHERIFF

*The snags from huge burns —
as far as the eye could see
looked like granite spears.*

— Andy Devine

HUCKLEBERRY PIE

Probably one of the most longed-for pies at our house. Ever so divine!

Mix together:

4 cups huckleberries

¾ cup sugar

2 rounded tablespoons flour

Make crust for a double crust pie. Pour berry mixture into crust, dot with butter and cover with crust. Cover outside edge with tin foil. Bake at 375° for 35-40 minutes or until pie bubbles in the middle.

NO FAIL WHITE BREAD

I am really hoping that all you young girls will try making this easy recipe.

6 cups warm water
3 tablespoons yeast
1 cup sugar
3 tablespoons salt
½ cup shortening
Flour

In a large mixing bowl dissolve yeast with sugar in the warm water. When yeast bubbles, add salt and begin adding in the flour. Mix in enough flour until dough starts to clean sides of the bowl. Pour dough out onto floured board and knead until dough all comes together. Knead in shortening. Dough will be smooth and elastic. Place dough into greased bowl; let rise until doubled. Punch down and shape into loaves of choice. Put into greased pans. Let rise again until doubled. Bake at 375° for 40-45 minutes.

PROVISIONS

Sent to a pioneer woman who had been on her own for nearly four years by the time her husband sent word that he was ready for the family to join him in the West:

40 lbs of desiccated vegetables and other items such as bacon, ham, dried beef, cod and fish.

600 lbs. of flour
300 lbs. of meal
50 lbs. of beans
100 lbs. of rice
50 lbs. of cheese
400 lbs. of sugar
20 gallons of syrup
50 lbs. of black tea
100 lbs. of coffee
400 lbs. of dried apples
400 lbs. of dried peaches
20 lbs. of salt

Elizabeth Simpson Bradshaw – 1850's
A widow, with five children, the youngest only 6 years of age, walked across the American prairie pushing all her family possessions in a handmade, wooden handcart. After much tribulation, more than could ever be told, Elizabeth, with all of her children still alive, arrived at her destination, the Salt Lake Valley. There in the West, she made her home, reared her children, and is honored by her posterity.

SWEET POTATO/SQUASH PIE

Make pastry for one-crust pie.

Beat together until smooth:

2 cups sweet potatoes or squash, (cooked; mashed or strained)

1 teaspoon salt

1 ½ cups milk; evaporated is best

3 eggs

1 cup sugar

1 teaspoon cinnamon

1 tablespoon butter, melted

2 teaspoons vanilla

Pour into pie pan with crust. Bake at 400° for 20 minutes; lower temperature to 350°. Bake for another 25-30 minutes until a knife inserted 1 inch from side of filling comes out clean. Cool. Serve with sweetened whipped cream.

Salt meat, from the "powdering tub," and ham smoked with treasured corn cobs, were served in every home. The Thanksgiving pies were made of bear's feet, dried pumpkins and maple sugar – with cornmeal crusts

SWEET POTATO ROLLS

1 ½ cups sweet potatoes, cooked and mashed

½ cup brown sugar, packed

3 packages yeast

½ cup butter, melted

3 ½ cups warm water, divided

4 teaspoons salt

10 cups flour, approximately

2 eggs, beaten

Cook and mash sweet potatoes. Set aside. Add yeast to 2 cups water and ½ cup brown sugar. Let stand until yeast mixture foams, then add butter, 1 ½ cups water, and 3 cups flour. Stir until well mixed. Add sweet potatoes, salt, and 2 beaten eggs. Mix well. Add flour until dough is stiff enough to knead. Knead until smooth and elastic; dough should be soft. Let rise until doubled. Shape each piece of dough into a ball and place in greased pans. Cover in warm place until doubled. Bake at 375° for 25-30 minutes. Butter tops of rolls when hot.

PEAR HONEY

A very good recipe from Billy Brisby.

4 cups ripe pears, peeled and chopped

4 cups sugar

1 (8oz.) can crushed pineapple, undrained

1 package pectin

Combine pears, sugar, and pectin; let set for one hour. Cook over medium heat, stirring constantly until pears are tender. Stir in pineapple and boil, stirring constantly, until syrup is almost like jelly. Pour pear honey into hot sterilized small jars and seal with hot sterilized lids.

Lambrecht's BUTTER "Famous for its Flavor" MILWAUKEE · CHICAGO

CARAMEL PECAN ROLLS

Who wouldn't want one of these prized rolls with a cup of coffee? Very easy and so yummy!

1 package of yeast	1 teaspoon salt
½ cup warm water	¼ cup butter
2 cups warm milk	1 egg, beaten
¼ cup sugar	5-6 cups flour

Dissolve yeast in warm water. Combine milk, sugar, and salt. Stir and allow to cool. Add yeast and water. Stir in beaten egg and flour. Put dough on a floured board and knead in ¼ cup butter until dough is smooth and elastic. Place in a greased bowl, grease top and cover. Let rise in a warm place. When doubled, turn dough out again on floured board. Roll out dough to ½ inch thickness. Spread with butter. Sprinkle with brown sugar and cinnamon over the butter. Roll from long end, like a jelly roll; cut in 1 inch slices. Bake at 375° for 30-35 minutes. Turn pan over onto rack. Do not overbake.

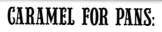

CARAMEL FOR PANS:

¼ cup butter	⅓ cup cream
½ cup Karo syrup	2 cups pecan halves
1 cup brown sugar	

Melt butter and divide between two 9x13 inch pans. Add half of the corn syrup, brown sugar, and cream to each pan. Sprinkle 1 cup pecans in each pan. Place rolls in pan. Let rise until doubled.

Think it was easier living during the Industrial Revolution? Here are some of the prices they were paying per week just to live:

1 bag of flour- $1.80

Small measure of potatoes daily at .17 per day- $1.19

¼ pound of tea-.38

1 quart of milk-.56

1 pound cheap coffee-.35

3 ½ pounds of sugar- $1.05

½ ration meats per week-$3.50

4 pounds of butter-$1.60

2 pounds of lard-.38

Dried apples for treats-.25

Vegetables-.50

Soap, starch, vinegar, pepper, salt, etc..-$1.00

2 bushels of coal-$1.36

Kerosene-.30

Sundries-.28

Rent-$4.00 a week

Total= $18.50 a week

*The average wage earner only made $16.00 per week.

To enjoy fruits of the land, with cream from the cow, was one of life's simple pleasures.

An account of the Massacre at Wounded Knee is difficult to relate because of the many opinions and statements regarding it. This narration has been written on that basis. While Indians were performing and preserving ceremonies (which they had been promised they could keep), the U.S. Government got worried that an ancient dance – the Ghost Dance ritual – was actually a war dance and may lead to rioting. Convinced that the dancers were preparing for battle, the War Department sent troops to occupy Indian camps. Meanwhile, Sitting Bull had just returned from Canada, with a promise of a pardon following the Battle at Little Bighorn. He was an advocate of the Ghost Dance. Reservation agents began to fear Sitting Bull's influence over other tribes, and agency police were sent to arrest him. Claiming he resisted arrest, the police murdered Sitting Bull and eight of his warriors. This began a chain of events comparable to Hitler's regime. Several Indians began a 150-mile week-long trek to reach the Pine Ridge Agency, proclaiming they wanted peace. A rumor was passed around that the Indians would end up in a camp worse than prison; the Indians were interrogated for hours by drinking soldiers. They demanded the Indians be stripped of their weapons and not be allowed to sleep. This only increased agitation in an intense and serious situation. A few of the Indians began singing Ghost Dance songs, and one of them threw dirt in a ceremonial act. This action was misunderstood by the soldiers as a sign of hostile aggression, and they immediately retaliated by spraying the unarmed Indians with bullets and cannon fire. The Indians, with only their bare hands to fight back, became part of a bloody chaos. Most were fatalities within 20 minutes of when it began. The firing lasted for several more hours, as soldiers hunted down Indians trying to escape. By mid-afternoon on December 29, 1890 the horrific slaughter ceased, leaving almost 300 men, women and children dead on the frozen banks of Wounded Knee Creek. When a burial party returned to Wounded Knee on New Year's Day, frozen bodies were strewn far and wide. In making a single burial pit, they found four live infants wrapped in their dead mothers' shawls. Later, the wounded and dying lay in the Pine Ridge Episcopal Church, a makeshift hospital. Above the pulpit hung a banner which read: Peace on Earth, Good Will to Men.

RICE PUDDING

A delightful treat, from Sharon Lindberg.

6 eggs, slightly beaten
2 cups milk
½ cup sugar
1 teaspoon vanilla

¼ teaspoon salt
1 ½ cups cooked rice
½ - ¾ cup dried fruit (craisins, raisins, cherries, strawberries, or apricots)

In ungreased two quart casserole dish mix eggs, milk, sugar, vanilla and salt. With a whip, beat until combined but not foamy. Stir in cooked rice and dried fruit. Place casserole dish in a larger pan with water up to one inch to steambake pudding. Bake at 325˚ for 30 minutes. Stir. Sprinkle with nutmeg and cinnamon. Bake for 20-30 minutes more until set. Remove from water and cool.

GROUND CHERRY PRESERVES

This recipe is very delicious on homemade biscuits.

2 pounds ground fresh cherries

1 cup water

4 cups sugar

Fresh-squeezed juice of 1 orange

Stir water and sugar together and bring to a boil. Add orange juice and ground cherries. Boil, stirring occasionally to keep preserves from sticking to the pan, until thick. Pour into sterilized jars, using lids, that have been soaking in hot water. Screw on lids to seal preserves. Enjoy!

BREAD PUDDING

Our daughter Lori says "this is the best bread pudding ever!"

1 loaf thick French bread or sourdough bread

1 cup brown sugar

1 ½ quarts half-n-half, milk or cream

¼ cup white chocolate

7 eggs

1 teaspoon ground cinnamon

1 teaspoon vanilla extract

GLAZE

2 cups powdered sugar

¼ cup white chocolate

1 teaspoon vanilla

½ cup milk

Mix well. Use to glaze pudding

Dice bread into large pieces and place in large mixing bowl. Add brown sugar and white chocolate. Mix eggs, half and half, cinnamon and vanilla, and pour into bread mixture. Mix until coated. Pour into lightly greased 13x9x2 pan. Place pan in larger pan filled with water so that you are steam baking the pudding. Bake at 350° for 30 minutes or until golden brown.

Firearms are second only to the
constitution in importance; they
are the peoples' liberty's teeth.
George Washington

FRIED RABBIT

When I was young we cooked rabbit. It actually tastes much like chicken. Experiment with different ways to cook rabbit; you might be quite surprised with the rabbit's tender mild flavor. Tame rabbits taste better than wild rabbits.

1 cup flour
1 teaspoon salt
½ teaspoon pepper
2-2 ½ lb. ready-to-cook Rabbit

Mix flour, salt and pepper. Coat rabbit pieces with flour mixture. In a skillet brown rabbit slowly in butter. Reduce heat; add 1 cup water and spices of choice. It is good with sprinkles of allspice, oregano, and a little lemon juice. Cook, covered, until tender, about 1 hour.

He who loses money, loses much.
He who loses a friend, loses much more.
He who loses faith, loses all.

– Eleanor Roosevelt

BUFFALO BURGERS

Many people say they prefer buffalo meat to beef. Give it a try!

Shape buffalo burger into 1 inch thick patties. Broil or grill. Cook 4-5 minutes on each side. Serve on burger buns with grilled onions.

BUFFALO BURGER BUNS

2 tablespoons yeast

2 cups warm water

1 tablespoon sugar

2 teaspoons salt

7 cups flour

1 egg white

2 teaspoons water

Soften yeast in water; add sugar. Allow yeast to bubble. Beat in salt and flour, one cup at a time, until dough is soft and smooth. Knead dough on a flat surface until smooth and elastic, adding more flour as needed. After dough has doubled in size, punch down and shape into hamburger buns. Place on a baking sheet that has been greased and sprinkled with cornmeal. Brush top of buns with egg white and water and sprinkle with cornmeal. Bake at 400° for 25 minutes.

"Fame is like a shaved pig with a greased tail, and it is only after it has slipped through the hands of some thousands, that some fellow, by mere chance, holds on to it."

— Davy Crockett

HOW TO RENDER LARD

Thanks alot Marty!

Marty Brosseau, a local butcher, gave me some pig fat to make lard. He tells me "the leaf lard is the best, this is the fat by the bacon." He refreshed me on how to render beautiful lard. When I was a young girl at home, and later in the first years of marriage, we butchered hogs and always had plenty of lard in our pantry. It is easy to make and always makes the best pie crust too! Melt down the fat in a slow oven (or now you can use a crock pot). When melted down, strain the grease through an old dish towel into a jar. It will thicken and be snowy white!

BBQ SAUSAGE ROUNDS

The secret to this yummy sausage is in the sauce. From Crystal Gillette's kitchen.

1 package smoked beef or kielbasa polish sausage, sliced
1 tablespoon butter
1 teaspoon garlic, minced
2-3 tablespoons honey
1 bottle Sweet Baby Ray's BBQ sauce

Brown sausage and garlic in butter in saucepan over medium heat; drizzle honey over sausage to coat, then add BBQ sauce and cook until sauce is heated through. Can be served by itself or on toothpicks with pickle and cheese as appetizer.

OLD WEST PIE CRUST

A very flaky good crust!

2 cups flour
½ teaspoon salt
¾ cup lard
Enough ice water to hold crust together

Roll out dough and cut into shapes using cookie cutters. Bake on cookie sheet until golden brown around edges at 400° for about 15 minutes. Remove from pan. Cool. Place cut-out pie crust pieces on top of thickened fruit. This crust recipe can also be used for a small 8" 2 crust pie.

WESTERN MARINATED TOMATOES

From Marlis Peters. This recipe is best in the summer with nice ripe fresh tomatoes.

3 tomatoes, ripe

1 sweet onion

1 teaspoon minced garlic, optional

2 tablespoons olive oil

½ teaspoon salt

1 teaspoon pepper

Slice tomatoes and onion onto a plate, add garlic and cover with oil. Sprinkle with salt and pepper. Refrigerate for one to two hours.

INDIAN ROASTED VEGETABLES

These vegetables will be on your table often once you try this recipe.

Cut vegetables of your choice into chunks or large pieces.

Spread veggies onto a heavy roasting pan, lined with foil that has been greased. Remember that higher density veggies (like carrots and potatoes) will take longer to roast. The oven heat sizzles and blisters the surface of the vegetables and this is what you want. Turn veggies at least once while cooking. Vegetables take around 45 minutes to cook in a hot 425° oven. Flavor with melted butter, cheese, lemon or fresh herbs before serving.

OLD WEST SWEET AND SOUR PORK CHOPS

Cecele Liner has made these pleasing pork chops for years and now her daughters and many others enjoy this easy recipe.

2 pork chops per person
Sauerkraut
Applesauce

Brown pork chops on each side. Place pork chops in a casserole baking pan. Cover pork chops with a layer of sauerkraut. Spread lightly with applesauce. On top of applesauce make another layer of pork chops, sauerkraut, and applesauce. Bake on 350˚ until pork is done – about 45 minutes-1 hour.

Near Ft. Boise the Indians made an attempt to attack our train and stampede the stock, but failed through the prompt action of my father, who ordered the teams unhitched and the wagons formed in a circle with the tongues of each run under the wagon just forward, making a strong barricade. The oxen were put inside, each driver standing by his own team. The women and children were also inside by the wagons. All the available men were outside standing with guns drawn. The captain walked out alone toward the Indians with his gun in one hand and a white flag in the other. He motioned the Indians not to come any nearer or his men would fire upon them. The Indians turned and ran away as fast as their horses could go. They had fine horses. The men were nude and painted.   –From an old diary

BBQ SALT

Good enough for any cowpoke or pretty lassie.

1 pound brown sugar
1 cup salt
1 oz. paprika
2 tablespoons black pepper

1 ½ teaspoons cayenne pepper
¼ teaspoon cinnamon
1 teaspoon garlic salt

Mix all ingredients together. Place in a tight container and keep refrigerated. Rub on meat before cooking.

When Napoleon's dreams of an American empire were defeated, he sold the Louisiana Territory to the U.S. for 15 million. President Jefferson bought 800,000 square miles between Missouri and The Rockies, doubling the size of our country.

TASTY TONGUE

I've cooked beef tongues for my husband, Sonny. This has to be true love! It actually doesn't look so conspicuously bad after it is cooked and the skin is peeled off! It is a delicacy and delicious in sandwiches. Every part of the cow can be used.

Wash the tongue in cold water. Salt tongue, then put it in a large pot, and cover well with plenty of cold water. A sliced onion can be added. Bring it to the boiling point, then slowly boil for 3-4 hours. Cook until tender (the exact time will vary according to the weight and the size of the tongue being boiled). Cool. Peel outside skin off and slice.

• Some people add ¼ cup of pickling spice while boiling.
• Buffalo tongue is also very good!

HOMINY FOR COWPOKES

My husband's mother, Grandma Rosie, grew hominy for her family for many years. It is quite a process! Very, very tasty.

2 tablespoons butter
2 large cans golden hominy
1 cup sour cream
½ teaspoon salt
Dash of pepper

Melt butter in a heavy cast iron skillet. Add drained hominy and sour cream. Season with salt and pepper. Heat until bubbling. Serve.

The hominy is harvested when it is hard on the cob. After picking and husking the corn, allow it to finish drying in a warm dry area. Shell the corn off the cob and let it soak with 2 teaspoons baking soda, in a pot of water, overnight. Remove hulls from corn. Rinse. Boil for at least an hour until corn is tender. If this process for home grown hominy is too much of a challenge, buy the cans at the store. Try this recipe!

LINE RIDER

As loneliness seeps into our souls, we struggle to endure the scorching heat daily, and endless bone-chilling nights, having only the labels on the lentils to remind us of our fragile humanity. Ride the line! Our cattle come first, pardner...ride the line.

COWBOY CHIPS

These yummy chips are hard to quit eating! So easy too!

12 flour tortillas

Olive oil

Seasoning of choice; chili powder, cinnamon and sugar, parmesan cheese...

Cut tortillas into 8 wedges or smaller. Brush large baking pan with oil. Arrange tortillas in a single layer on pan. Brush the tortillas with oil. Sprinkle with desired seasoning. Bake at 325° until crisp and lightly browned.

COWPUNCHER STEW

Eating was the main item of business back in the good ol' days. There was little conversation. Stew was then and is now a very hearty meal.

2 pounds beef stew meat, cut into 1 inch cubes

1 ½ cups strongly brewed coffee

2 tablespoons molasses

1 teaspoon salt

1 teaspoon garlic salt

⅛ teaspoon cayenne pepper

Flour, enough to coat meat

In a CAST IRON POT brown meat on all sides, after coating it with flour and salt. Stir in coffee, molasses, garlic salt, and cayenne pepper. Cover; simmer over low heat until meat is tender, about 1 ½ hours.

Add:

1 ½ cups water

5 carrots, cut into ½ inch slices

2 onions, cut into large pieces

3 potatoes, peeled and cut up

Cook about 30 minutes, adding more water if needed. Thicken with ¼ cup water and 3 tablespoons flour. Cook and stir until mixture is thickened and bubbly. Serve.

CORN MUFFINS

These muffins are different, but sooo good! Serve with stew, soup or chili.

1 cup flour

1 cup cornmeal

2 tablespoons sugar

2 tablespoons baking powder

½ teaspoon baking soda

½ teaspoon salt

1 can cream style corn

½ cup buttermilk

1 egg

2 tablespoons butter, melted

In a bowl, combine flour, cornmeal, sugar, baking powder, soda, and salt. In another bowl, whisk together corn, buttermilk, egg, and melted butter. Add to dry ingredients. Stir until dry ingredients are moistened. Do not beat too much. Makes 12 large muffins. Bake for 20 minutes at 375˚. Do not over-bake muffins. Serve warm.

In the early days, whole eggs were placed in huge crocks. Placed layer upon layer with an inch of salt between the layers, the eggs would then be stored in a cave or cellar.

FRIED CHICKEN

We all love fried chicken, especially if cooked at home. This is an especially good way to cook chunks of fish also.

1 frying chicken, cut up

Lemon juice

1 ½ cups flour

1 ½ cups dried bread
   crumbs

2 teaspoons salt

1 teaspoon pepper

1 ½ cups half and half

Wash and dry chicken. Brush with fresh lemon juice. Combine flour, crumbs, salt and pepper and coat chicken lightly. Dip in half and half and again in flour and crumbs. I like to fry chicken in Crisco, about ½ inch in a cast iron skillet. Brown chicken a few pieces at a time, over medium heat. When all is browned, pour off some of the grease and reduce heat, cover and cook for 20 minutes. Uncover and cook another 20 minutes. So good to take to a picnic.

LEMON DILL SALAD

Recipe from Judy Toivonen. She offers the following information, " This salad is for garlic lovers. Super simple. Light and refreshing good summer salad and great for a quick BBQ. Mix together and enjoy."

Red potatoes, cooked, cooled and
   halved or quartered

Mayonnaise

1 package of organic baby dill, finely chopped

2 tablespoons lemon juice

1 heaping tablespoon minced garlic

2 green onions, chopped

½ cup celery, chopped

SALMON DIP

A zippy tasty dip for crackers. Clarence and Sherry Deel made this quick and easy dip for us when they came west. They report that the spices can be less or more depending on your liking.

1 (14.7oz.) can Salmon, drained well

½ cup Miracle Whip

¼ cup horseradish

⅛ cup parsley flakes

4 dashes Texas Pete hot sauce

1 tablespoon minced garlic

1 tablespoon jalapeno juice

Mix together and chill. Fresh cooked salmon may also be used.

Following the wide Columbia River, the immigrants traveled on toward The Dalles. "Loaded up our boat and left. Paid $17 for freight and passage...came down about fifteen miles and landed. We buried a child which we found upon the bank of the river, drowned."
— David S. Maynard, diary 1850

SALMON CASSEROLE

This recipe is from Bodil Bergbom's family. Bodil was an exchange student in America and she made this recipe for her host parents, Hollie and Kevin Rose. It is very similar to the Salmon Loaf my family has made for years. You'll love it if you enjoy salmon. Hollie felt it should go in this western recipe book and I agree.

6-8 potatoes

Salmon, (approx. 2 lbs., cooked or canned)

4 eggs

1 ½ cups milk

2 onions

1 tablespoon butter, melted

Parsley and pepper to taste

Bake at 475˚. Slice the raw potatoes very thin. Chop onion. Layer potatoes, onions, and cooked salmon in a deep pan (9x12). Whisk eggs and milk. Add melted butter, parsley, and pepper over the top. Bake 35-40 minutes.

BUFFALO JERKY

Of course beef or venison can also be used.
The guys say this is a great recipe from Basil Rotschy.

3-4 pounds round steak,
    cut into strips
6 cups apple cider
2 cups water
3 cups soy sauce
¼ cup salt
¼ cup brown sugar
⅛ cup onion salt

Let this mixture sit for 10-15 hours on meat strips. Remove meat strips and pat dry with paper towels. Arrange in single layers on racks in shallow baking pans. Thickness of the meat will determine the time needed to dry. Repeat until all strips are dried. Smoke until jerky is done in an outside smoker. If using an inside oven, bake at 300° for 50 to 60 minutes or until dry. You can sprinkle with coarse pepper if desired. Cool in an airtight container. Can be refrigerated for at least 2 weeks.

WILLIAM F. "BUFFALO BILL" CODY

1846-1917

Every once in a while when the kingpin falls just right, stars align perfectly and simply by luck of the draw a great man is born! William Cody (Buffalo Bill) was charmed and molded to become the epitome of the Great Western Legend. By the age of 14 he had already ridden for the Pony Express and worked as a prospector, trapper and drover. Buffalo Bill played "Cowboys and Indians" professionally, working as a scout for several campaigns against Indians, earning himself a Congressional Medal of Honor for bravery. Buffalo Bill's infectious excitement and compelling charisma won the hearts of wealthy men coming West on the railroad, who had him serve as a guide for royalty and government officials. Later, Buffalo Bill headed East and began producing Wild West Shows, traveling all over the country with Annie Oakley, and his good friend, Wild Bill Hickock, and others. They wowed audiences with enactments of the Wild West. Buffalo Bill died at the ripe old age of 72, a wealthy man with everlasting fame. Dime novelists loved writing about William Cody because after all, he was a true story book hero!

PRIME RIB ROAST

Most any cowboy will like this mouth-watering meat. Darci Frazier shared this grand recipe. Easier than it sounds! "Me, make prime rib?" Sure you can, cowgirl.

8 pound prime rib roast
1 box rock salt or sea salt (Darci prefers Morton's Kosher coarse ground salt)
Garlic powder to taste

Take the roast out of refrigerator a few hours before cooking to allow it to come to room temperature. When ready to cook, sprinkle roast with garlic. Pour salt into a bowl and add enough water (approximately 1 cup) to form a paste. Coat the bottom of a roasting pan (where the roast will sit) with some of the paste and place the roast in the pan. Then cover the entire roast by patting on the remaining salt paste. Cook at 325° for approximately 2½ hours or to desired doneness. When done, the salt will have formed a crust that is easily removed to reveal a delicious, tender roast!

PRIME RIB

The best prime rib I've ever tasted was prepared by our daughter Cheri. It was very tender and tasty.

Rub roast with Good Seasons Italian dressing.

Coat with:
2 parts coarse ground pepper
1 part granulated garlic
1 part Lawry's season salt
A pinch of: sage
                white pepper
                basil

Cook fat side up at 325° for about 4 hours.

WYATT EARP

Wyatt Earp is best known for his participation in the controversial "Gunfight at the O.K. Corral," which took place at Tombstone, Arizona, on October 26, 1881. In this legendary Old West clash, Wyatt Earp, his brothers Virgil and Morgan, and Doc Holliday faced off with Ike and Billy Clanton and Tom and Frank McLaury. The big shootout and the bloody battle that followed, along with Wyatt Earp's storytelling, resulted in Wyatt Earp getting a reputation as being one of the Old West's toughest and deadliest western heroes. There are many novels and films portraying his life. How much is true is up to you to decide.

GERMAN CHOCOLATE CAKE

Our daughter, Lori Anne, makes this cake often...for someone. When we are the lucky recipients, we share it with our company and there are so many oh's and ah's.

1 (4oz.) package Baker's German
   Sweet Chocolate
½ cup water
2 cups flour
1 teaspoon baking soda
¼ teaspoon salt

1 cup butter, softened
2 cups sugar
4 eggs, separated
1 teaspoon vanilla
1 cup buttermilk

Microwave chocolate and water on high 1½ to 2 minutes or until chocolate is almost melted, stirring after 1 minute. Stir until chocolate is completely melted. Mix dry ingredients together, set aside. Beat butter and sugar together until fluffy. Add egg yolks, one at a time, beating well after each. Blend in melted chocolate and vanilla. Add flour mixture alternately with buttermilk, beating until well blended after each addition. Beat egg whites until stiff peaks form. Gently stir into batter. Pour evenly into 3 well greased and floured 9 inch cake pans. Bake 25-30 minutes at 350° or until a toothpick inserted in the center comes out clean. Cool on wire racks in pans for 15 minutes.

COCONUT PECAN FROSTING:

4 egg yolks
1 can evaporated milk
1 teaspoon vanilla
1 ½ cups sugar

¾ cup butter
2 ½ cups flaked coconut
2 cups pecans, chopped

Beat egg yolks, milk, and vanilla in a saucepan with a wire whisk until well blended. Add sugar and butter. Cook on medium heat until thickened and golden brown, stirring constantly. Remove from heat. Add coconut and nuts. Cool and spread on the cake.

"It does not require many words to speak the truth." -Chief Joseph

ON WASHING DAY

"I have seen her rub and scrub,
On the washboard in the tub,
While the baby sopped in suds,
Rolled and tumbled in the duds;
Or was paddling in the pools,
With old scissors stuck in spools;
She still humming of her friend
Who would keep her to the end."

This is part of Ironquill's "The Washerwoman's
Song." It told the story of a woman, a widow who
sang of a savior who would keep her to the end,
singing it while she did her daily chores.

SOAP

Oh, how we used to make soap when I was a child! Mother learned from Aunt Lizzie the correct amounts of lye to use. I wish I had that recipe for soap. I wonder if we realize how fortunate we are to stop at the store for a box of soap. We waited until we butchered the hogs to have ample fat for the soap. This recipe is for 9 pounds of soap and is a very old recipe.

Fats – use only fats free from impurities and water.
Water – use rain water if possible. Never use hard water.
Lye – use the best quality of lye you can buy.
6 pounds fat • 2 ½ pints water • 1 can lye

Put water in a stone jar. Pour in lye and then put on the cover. Shake the jar to dissolve the lye. Melt down the fat. Cool lye to 70° before adding fat which should be cooled to about the consistency of honey. Pour the lye into the fat, slowly, stirring the mixture steadily in one direction. When the mixture becomes as thick as salad dressing pour out at once into a pasteboard box lined with a cotton cloth wrung out of warm water. This box should be kept in a warm room free from drafts (on a table). Cover it with a rug or old blanket to keep in the heat. Too much lye will make crumbly soap.

76

BBQ BAKED BEANS

Great family recipe from Marlis Peters and Wayne Oltman.

2 pounds ground beef
1 small bottle barbeque sauce
1 can kidney beans, 15 oz.
1 can black beans, 15 oz.
1 can pinto beans, 15 oz.
1 can pork and beans, 15 oz.
1 small onion, chopped
1 can black eyed peas, 15 oz.
1 can white navy beans, 15 oz.
1 can lima beans, 15 oz.
¼ cup ketchup
3 cloves garlic, minced (optional)
1 teaspoon salt
1 teaspoon black pepper

Brown ground beef in skillet; add onions and garlic and cook until softened. Drain all the canned beans except the pork and beans. Put all ingredients in a large pot and simmer for 2 hours. Serve.

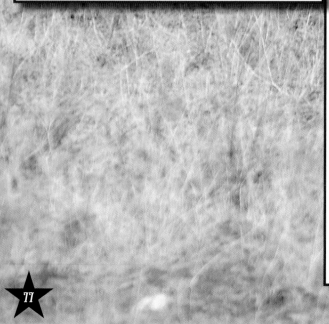

HOT BEAN SALAD

A blue star for this recipe from Merle Moore. This makes a delicious accompaniment to any BBQ.

1 pound regular sausage
1 (28 oz.) can baked beans
1 (16 oz.) can lima beans
1 (16 oz.) can green beans, regular cut
1 (16 oz.) can yellow beans, regular cut
1 (16 oz.) can kidney beans
1 (10 ¾ oz.) can tomato soup
¾ cup diced celery
½ cup chopped onion
½ cup brown sugar, packed
1 tablespoon dry mustard
Bacon strips to cover

Preheat oven to 375°. Brown the sausage and drain, saving fat to sauté the celery and onions. While the celery and onions are sautéing, drain the lima, green and yellow beans. Partially drain the kidney beans. Mix everything together and pour into a 4 quart baking dish. Cover with bacon strips. Bake one hour at 375°. Can be mixed together one day, refrigerated, and then baked the next day. Also freezes well. When ready to bake just thaw and follow baking instructions above.

On June 14th, 1777, Betsy Ross presented George Washington with our first flag.
[Ge]orge chose the colors: red for courage, white for liberty, and blue for loyalty. Only
[th]e stars have changed — to 50. May God continue to bless America and you and me!

Calvin Coolidge is the only U.S. President born on the 4th of July — in Plymouth, Vermont, in 1872.

Associate with men of good quality if you esteem your own reputation; for it is better to be alone than in bad company.
— George Washington

CANDIED PARSNIPS

Now this is some good eating! Sonny grows parsnips and we get people to try this dish. Most everyone is surprised at what they've been missing in their diet. The local markets have parsnips year round.

Cook the amount of parsnips you desire; cut into pieces before cooking, do not peel. Cook until tender. Cool and peel off skin. Cut into thin slices. Place slices in a pan. Sprinkle with brown sugar, salt and pepper. Pour a ½ cup of melted butter over all. Bake for 30 minutes at 375°.

WINTER SQUASH

My dear husband, Sonny, loves to grow lots of squash. We enjoy it very much in the cold winter time.

Boil or bake squash until tender, remove from skin and mash. Add salt, pepper, butter and brown sugar to taste. Pour mixture into a 2 quart baking dish. For an extra treat sprinkle crushed Ritz crackers with a little melted butter over the top of the squash. Bake at 350° for 45 minutes.

PAN FRIED CABBAGE

Most all cowboys loved cooked cabbage!

2 tablespoons bacon drippings
1 tablespoon sugar
1 head cabbage, shredded
½ teaspoon salt
¼ cup vinegar
Dash cayenne pepper
¼ cup water

Heat drippings in skillet. Add cabbage, vinegar, water, sugar, salt, and cayenne. Cook over medium heat stirring occasionally, until cabbage is lightly browned but still crisp, about 10-12 minutes. Serve hot.

LONG-HORN ROAST BEEF

Who doesn't enjoy a good roasted beef? Juicy and flavorful. Leftovers for sandwiches or hash! Season the meat with salt and pepper. I use garlic salt lavishly. This seems to make the roast more tender. Roasts can be cooked in a frozen state.

Add about 1 inch of water; cover your roaster with a lid. Cook at 350° until browned and juicy. Extra good with garlic cloves, onions and mushrooms.

lie and you lose yourself. – Hopi

WESTERN HASH

Our children were raised on hash. My husband furnished us with an abundance of wild meat. I found hash to be the best way to hide the wild taste for me. I usually fried a couple dozen eggs to go with the menu of venison hash.

Pull out the grinder, if you don't have one, a lot of garage sales and maybe Goodwill has them. Cut up equal quantities of roast or canned meat and fresh spuds. Grind the cut up pieces with an onion. Season with salt and pepper. It is extra good to moisten the hash with half and half or leftover gravy. Brown in a skillet until crispy. I use butter and olive oil. It is excellent heated the next day, also.

CHERI'S SUPERB SALSA

A true winner!

10 large ripe Roma tomatoes
1 large white onion
4 large garlic cloves
2 medium/large jalapeno peppers
2 medium/large serrano peppers
2-4 tablespoons chopped fresh cilantro
2 teaspoons salt

Cut out stem section of 5 tomatoes and cook whole. Chunk up ½ onion, 2 cloves of garlic, and 2 of each pepper. Place in medium saucepan with one inch of water. Add 2 tablespoons chopped cilantro. Bring to boil, turn temperature down and simmer until all veggies are soft. (Don't let water boil dry!) Set aside to cool. Meanwhile, chop remaining tomatoes, and add onion in ¼ inch size pieces. Press remaining garlic, and finely chop peppers. Put into large bowl. Skin cooked tomatoes, and place all cooked ingredients into blender and puree. Pour into bowl with mixture. Add salt and remaining cilantro. Enjoy!

• Cheri says "This salsa is fairly hot. Play around with it! Makes a great base salsa for other ingredients such as mango, peaches, nectarines, corn, avocado, etc...Cooked and cut asparagus is also excellent! I make this salsa often and it vanishes quickly. It goes great on eggs, Mexican dishes or served with chips. Note: sometimes if salsa is too runny, or tomatoes aren't ripe enough, 1 large can of tomato sauce can be added for richer flavor."

SALSA VERDE-GREEN SALSA

Our daughter, Lori got this recipe and the salsa for us to try from Irene Sarmiento. Everyone said it was good!

1 pound tomatillos
4-6 jalapenos for mild to medium, 8 for really hot
¼ of 1 large onion
3 cloves of garlic
3-4 whole sprays of cilantro

Remove papery skin from tomatillos and wash them. Remove stems from jalapenos. Put tomatillos and jalapenos with onions and garlic into a sauce pan with water to cover. Boil for 5-6 minutes and turn off heat and allow to cool. Put the cooked mixture into a blender with cilantro and blend until smooth. Add a little water to thin out if desired and salt to taste. Green salsa is great on pork or in enchiladas or tacos.

Small in stature, descending from Spanish strays, no animal or man alone could outdistance or outsmart our mustang. Never failing their riders, with sheer orneriness, these hardy horses carved a trail into our frontier, unshod and overworked, and helped make our West what it came to be.

PEACH RASPBERRY SALSA

This is a very good summer picnic salsa with a little zip. Serve with your choice of chips.

3 large fresh peaches, diced

¾ cup raspberry jam

1 tablespoon fresh lemon juice

½ teaspoon crushed dried red pepper

Stir ingredients all together in a small bowl.

CHEDDAR BISCUITS

These yummy biscuits are quite tasty. Recipe from Judy Tikka.

1 ½ cups flour
½ cup white whole wheat flour
2 teaspoons baking powder
¼ teaspoon baking soda
¼ teaspoon salt
3 tablespoons plus 1 teaspoon
    chilled butter
1 teaspoon Johnny's Seasoning Salt
¾ cup buttermilk
¾ cup shredded sharp cheddar cheese

Combine dry ingredients. Cut in butter with a pastry blender until mixture resembles coarse meal. Add buttermilk and cheese. Drop ¼ cup portions of the dough onto an ungreased baking sheet using an ice cream scoop. Bake at 400° for 12-17 minutes or until the tops of the biscuits are light brown. You may use low-fat buttermilk to cut out some fat and calories.

NAVY BEANS AND HAM

This is an old stand-by, a good way to use leftover ham, bone and all.

2 pounds navy beans

4 quarts water

3 cups ham, with bone

1 onion, chopped

Salt and pepper

2 tablespoons butter

Wash navy beans in water. Combine beans in a large pot with hot water, ham, salt, and pepper. Boil about 2 ½ hours, with a lid on the top. Brown onion in butter and add to beans after they've boiled a couple hours.

BROWN BREAD

This is a no yeast quick-bread.
Very old-fashioned and satisfying.

²/₃ cup brown sugar

3 tablespoons butter

½ cup molasses

3 cups whole wheat flour

1 cup white flour

1 teaspoon baking soda

1 teaspoon baking powder

1 ½ teaspoons salt

2 ½ cups buttermilk

1 cup raisins

1 cup walnuts, chopped

Mix in order given. Grease 2 medium size
loaf pans. Bake at 325° for 45 min.- 1 hour.

BUFFALO CHILI

A Western cowboy chili with a nourishing taste.
Recipe from Cheryl Crume. She says her husband
loved to take this on his hunting trip every year.

1 pound ground buffalo or beef

1 medium chopped onion

1 6oz. can tomato paste

1 can French onion soup

1 cup dried red kidney beans, soaked overnight

4 cups water or canned tomatoes

1 ½ tablespoons chili powder

1 ½ teaspoons salt

1 teaspoon garlic powder

1 teaspoon sugar

A few shakes of Tabasco

Put everything in a slow cooker on high for 8-10 hours.

Better to remain silent and be thought a fool than to speak out and remove all doubt. – Abraham Lincoln

89

ANNIE OAKLEY

Who says only outlaws and tough men were good with a gun? Well, sir, they'd never met Annie Oakley! Nine-year-old Annie was already shooting game and by the time she was 15 she could outshoot most men. Just like a woman, she set out to impress others with this fine talent. Annie Oakley joined Buffalo Bill's Wild West Show, impressing audiences all over the country with her almost perfect marksmanship. Annie Oakley... one of the West's most famous women...there's no doubt about it!

BRIAN'S LEAN/MEAN CHILI

Recipe from Brian Rich. He says "It serves 25 people or 2 fat guys."

In a Dutch oven combine:

1 ½ lbs. ground beef

2 tablespoons olive oil

2-3 teaspoons salt

1 green pepper, chopped

1 red or yellow pepper, chopped

2 medium onions, chopped

2 packages McCormick Chili Dry Mix

4 to 6 grinds fresh black pepper

Cook over medium heat, stirring occasionally until cooked through.
Add:

4-6 minced garlic cloves

2 tablespoons grated garlic from a jar

6 large celery stalks, chopped

2- (28oz.) cans tomatoes, finely diced

1-(15oz.) can tomato sauce

¼ cup cilantro leaves, finely diced (no stems)

3-4 tablespoons Texas Pete's Hot Sauce

Simmer, stirring occasionally, about an hour, until flavors blend
and vegetables are cooked. You can add 2 cans chili beans
(hot) if you like. Serve hot with grated cheddar cheese, sour
cream, saltines, and extra hot sauce. There are many opinions
on how to cook chili. Usually you should double the batch of
chili you choose to make! Leftover chili is even better the next day.

In the beginning of the 17th Century, the tiny Mayflower brought to America 102 English Pilgrims who had left their country to find religious freedom. Behind these first settlements, reaching out towards the west, a vast primitive forest loomed up like a wall of green. The wall went to the setting sun. And west the settlers came, they came to the last frontier.

CHICKEN ENCHILADAS

A favorite recipe from our daughter, Lori.

1 (28oz.) can green chili enchilada sauce

1 (10 ¾ oz.) can cream of chicken soup

1 cup sour cream

1 small can chopped green chilies

1 cup cream or evaporated milk

8 cups cooked, cubed chicken

4 cups grated cheese of choice

9 flour tortilla shells

11x15 baking pan (larger than a 9x13)

Mix first five ingredients together. Mix 2 cups of sauce with cubed chicken in a bowl. Divide this combination evenly onto nine tortilla shells. Sprinkle with 2 cups of grated cheese and roll up tortilla shells. Pour 2 cups sauce into the bottom of pan. Place rolled up enchiladas on top of the sauce in pan. Pour the remaining sauce over the enchilada. Lastly sprinkle the remaining 2 cups of grated cheese over the complete pan. Bake at 400° for ½ hour. Serve with your favorite chips and salsa.

SALSA ROJA-RED SALSA

A great salsa from Pedro Bernabe.

4 large red tomatoes

3 jalapenos

4 cloves garlic

½ small onion

Cilantro

Chop in food processor until chunky, not smooth. Chop ¼ to ½ bunch of cilantro and stir into salsa. Salt to taste. Enjoy! Great on eggs, meat, anything...

SALSA VERDE-GREEN SALSA

OLD TIME FRIED CLAMS

What a treat! These delicious clams are fun to dig and so tender to eat. Can you imagine what Lewis and Clark thought when they found razor clams?

Dip whole clean clams in flour, then in beaten egg with a little milk, next in fine cracker crumbs. Fry in ½ inch of oil until golden brown (about 5 minutes). Drain on absorbent paper. Serve with lemon and tartar sauce.

SHRIMP BOIL

You cannot beat this scrumptious great pleasure! We were served this shrimp boil in North Carolina. Mary and Stan Sneeden, very favorite cousins, prepared dinner for many of us at their beach house. When you have a crowd over, this is a must! I'm sure Lewis and Clark would have served this out west if they had brought along a big kettle! Don't you think? Delicious, it is really hard to limit your intake!

Fill a large pot, (your canner will work great,) half full of water. Add 4 tablespoons of Old Bay Seafood Seasoning. Bring to a boil.

Next: Add four pounds Kielbasa sausage cut in 2 inch slices. Bring to a boil.

Next: Add 3 pounds of small red potatoes. Bring to a boil.

Next: Add 5 large sweet onions, cut in half. Bring to a boil.

Next: Add 32 ears of corn, if large, cut in half; count each half as an ear. Bring to boil.

Next: Add 7 pounds of shrimp, de-headed and uncooked, with shell. When shrimp turn pink, shut off burner and allow to sit for 5 minutes.

Drain off juices. Put food into large bowls or on newspaper in the middle of tables. Have plenty of butter, salt, pepper, and cocktail sauce. Start shelling shrimp! Yummy!

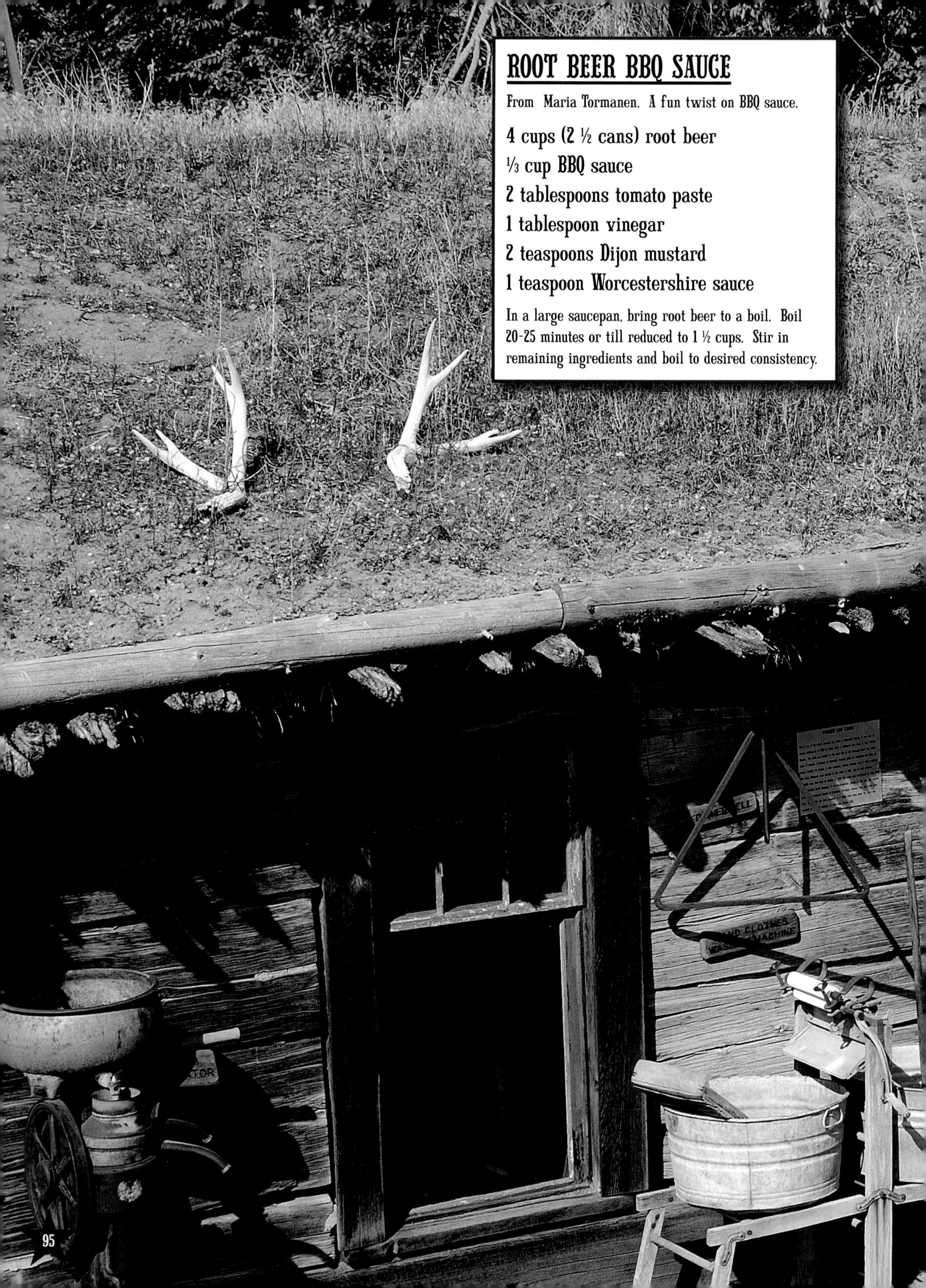

ROOT BEER BBQ SAUCE

From Maria Tormanen. A fun twist on BBQ sauce.

4 cups (2 ½ cans) root beer

⅓ cup BBQ sauce

2 tablespoons tomato paste

1 tablespoon vinegar

2 teaspoons Dijon mustard

1 teaspoon Worcestershire sauce

In a large saucepan, bring root beer to a boil. Boil 20-25 minutes or till reduced to 1 ½ cups. Stir in remaining ingredients and boil to desired consistency.

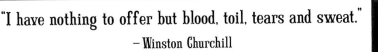

"I have nothing to offer but blood, toil, tears and sweat."
– Winston Churchill

HOME BREWED ROOT BEER

First you need to buy root beer extract. Now, find a bottle sealer with the caps or use corks. Find what you'll need before starting. Pour 1 bottle of root beer extract over 4 pounds of sugar and mix well. Dissolve this mixture into 5 gallons of lukewarm water. Mix ½ teaspoon dry yeast into ½ cup warm water with some sprinkles of sugar to make the yeast work. Let stand until dissolved. Add yeast mixture to the water, extract and sugar. Stir well and bottle immediately. Fill bottles to within ½ inch of the top. Place bottles on their sides away from drafts until effervescent (fizzy). It should be ready to drink in approximately 5 days after bottling (longer in cool weather). Then set bottles in a cool dry place. Just before drinking, refrigerate bottles for a short time to make the beverage sparkling. Make sure bottles are clean before making the root beer. Finished beverage will contain some sediment from the yeast and particles of the pure ingredients that give flavor and make the root beer tasty. A slight yeast flavor may be detected.

Hudson's Bay Company's bead value for a "made beaver:"

- Six Hudson's Bay beads
- Three light blue Padre (crow) beads
- Two larger transparent blue beads

One ordinary riding horse =
- 8 buffalo robes
- 1 gun and 100 loads ammunition
- 1 carrot of tobacco weighing 3 lbs.
- 15 eagle feathers
- 10 weasel skins (ermine)
- 5 tipi poles
- 1 skin shirt and leggings, decorated with human hair and quills

One buffalo robe =
- 3 metal knives
- 25 loads of ammunition
- 1 large metal kettle
- 3 dozen iron arrow points
- ½ yard of calico

One fine racing horse = 10 guns
One fine buffalo horse = several pack animals
Three buffalo robes = 1 white blanket
Four buffalo robes = 1 scarlet Hudson's Bay blanket
Five buffalo robes = 1 bear claw necklace
Thirty beaver pelts = 1 keg of rum (diluted)
Ten ermine pelts = 100 elk teeth

RED GRAVY

Shannon Lindberg's great grandmother, Lillian Holmes made this Texan gravy. It has been passed down in the family.

¼ cup Bacon grease

¼ cup chopped onions

¼ cup flour

2 (8 oz.) cans tomato sauce

Salt, pepper, and chili powder to taste

In a cast iron skillet heat the grease. Stir in chopped onions; brown them nicely. Stir the flour into the grease and onions; Keep stirring until the flour is just starting to brown. Then slowly stir in tomato sauce. If you want gravy to be a little thinner, add a little water. Season with salt, pepper and chili powder. Simmer for a few minutes. Serve over home fried potatoes. Some people like the red gravy over biscuits.

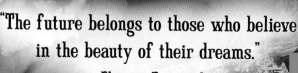

"The future belongs to those who believe in the beauty of their dreams."
–Eleanor Roosevelt

CHEESY MASHED POTATOES

We've made these filling spuds since I was a child. You can add crisp bacon pieces, grilled and chopped onions, garlic, sour cream, cream cheese, parmesan cheese, hot peppers. Cook and mash the amount of potatoes you will need using salt, pepper, and hot milk. Pour potatoes in a casserole dish and top with grated cheddar cheese. Bake in the oven until cheese is melted and starting to brown. Serve.

CABBAGE PATCH STEW

After Candy Wallace bought my other book, THE OLD FARMHOUSE KITCHEN, she called me to say, "Every recipe in the book is something I would make and I've made several recipes and they have been a great hit." This soup is hearty and so good.

2 pounds lean ground beef

2 cups cabbage, shredded

1 large onion, chopped

1 cup celery, chopped

2 cups water

2 teaspoons salt

1 tablespoon Worcestershire sauce

1 tablespoon sugar

1 tablespoon chili powder

1 (28 oz.) can tomatoes

3 cans (15 ½ ounces) kidney beans, with juice

Brown meat; add vegetables. Cook until clear and wilted. Add water, salt, seasonings, tomatoes and beans. Simmer for ½ hour.

Saluting The Kernel!

There is no better way to capture the quintessential flavors of the season than with the summertime's fresh corn. Corn always has an even number of rows on each ear. For every kernel of corn on the cob, there is one strand of silk.

SWEET CORN BREAD PUDDING

Wow! Our neighbor Merle Moore made this good recipe for us. She says "Bob and I love this as a side dish with Thanksgiving dinner. I bake it in the morning then reheat it while the turkey is resting."

½ cup onion, finely diced

2 tablespoons unsalted butter

½ teaspoon thyme

½ teaspoon rosemary

1 (15oz.) can cream style corn

1 cup heavy whipping cream

2 eggs

1 teaspoon baking powder

½ cup yellow, stone ground, whole grain corn meal

½ cup shredded parmesan cheese

1 teaspoon salt (I prefer Kosher salt)

Ground black pepper to taste

2 cups French bread cut into one inch cubes

Preheat oven to 350˚. Sauté onions with butter and herbs over medium low heat in a 10 inch oven safe skillet until soft. Combine corn, cream, eggs, baking powder, cornmeal, parmesan cheese, salt and pepper in a large mixing bowl. Add cubed bread and mix gently to combine. Pour batter into skillet, on top of the onion mixture. Bake 40-50 minutes or until set (time will vary depending on individual oven). Cool slightly before serving.

CORN

The physical endurance of the colonists was almost superhuman. It was the result of a plain diet, centering around corn, the great sustaining food.

BANDANA

Tho I'm just a lil red kerchief
...A cloth square, rather small,
My uses for the cowboy...
Stack up real tall!

Hot scorching days, I soak the sweat
That drips from weary brows.
Bitter cold nights, necks are wrapped
As we go round up them cows!

I'm especially great at wiping things...
I can snap a fly on the run!
As a wash rag, I come in real handy
At chowtime...when day is done.

BUCKAROO NACHOS

2 pounds browned, drained
    hamburger with added taco seasoning
2 large packages of tortilla chips
1 jar of Tostitos Con Queso cheese sauce
1 (1 lb.) package of shredded Mexican cheese
1 (6 oz.) large can black olives,
    drained and sliced
1 small jar sliced jalapeno peppers, drained

Layer two large cookie sheets with chips, then on top of chips dollop teaspoons of Con Queso, taco meat, olives, and jalapenos and lastly sprinkle shredded cheese lightly on top of that. Depending on the size of crowd, add more chips for another layer. Heat at 375° till cheese is melted through but before chips start to brown. If double layering, eating right away is recommended. After heating pans, you may dollop the top with salsa, sour cream, guacamole, shredded lettuce, sliced green onions and freshly diced tomato; or, if you choose serve all above ingredients buffet style.

"From the sweet grass to the packin' house, we're all travelers in this life; traveling between the eternities."

SADDLE BAG PULL-APART BREAD

Recipe from my sister Linda Kysar, one of the best cooks I know.

1 cup warm water

1 package yeast

2 tablespoons sugar

1 teaspoon salt

2 tablespoons butter

1 egg

3 ½ cups flour

⅓ cup melted butter for dipping

Dissolve yeast in water; add remaining ingredients; knead until smooth. Roll to 15x12 rectangle. Cut dough into diamond shapes by cutting into 1 ½ strips diagonally. Dip each piece in melted butter and layer in prepared pan. Sprinkle each layer with a little dill weed. Cover and let rise until double the size. About 1 hour. Bake 20-25 minutes at 350°. Prepare pan by greasing 12 cup fluted tube pan (Bundt); sprinkle with dill weed.

MAPLE COOKIES

Our daughter Cheri served us these tender delicious cookies on one of our trips to Montana.

½ cup butter

½ cup shortening

½ cup brown sugar

½ cup granulated sugar

1 egg

1 teaspoon vanilla

2 cups flour

½ teaspoon baking soda

½ teaspoon salt

Cream butter, shortening, and both sugars together. Add egg and vanilla. Mix well. Add dry ingredients. Roll dough into small balls. Pat cookies down to about 2 inches across. Bake at 350° for about 8-10 minutes. Do not over-bake. Remove from pan and cool. Frost with maple glaze.

MAPLE GLAZE

Melt ¼ cup butter until golden brown. Blend in 1 cup sifted powdered sugar and a few drops of maple flavoring. Stir in 1 to 2 tablespoons hot water until icing spreads smoothly.

Let your mind wander back a bit –
when times were real and true.
To a land that was conquered with guns
and spurs, branding irons, and a good lasso.

– Andy Devine

BILLY THE KID -$500 REWARD OFFERED FOR CAPTURE-

(William Bonny) 1860-1881

The Irish immigrant named William Bonny was left motherless at 14 years. He found himself alone in a merciless world at 17 years young. A loner by nature, Billy teetered on the brink of violence and eventually became a particularly vicious killer who tortured our west. By the fall of 1877, two deputies were shot down, which triggered the fatal quirk in the Kid. Forgetting compassion, lacking self-control, Billy rode with no regard to his victims. By 1879, submitting to a short arrest, the Kid slipped his cuffs off due to small hands and large wrists and took his leave. The Kid remained at large for another year, finding himself on the Pecos River, where he developed his fateful friendship with Beaver Saloon's bartender, Pat Garrett. Longing for a clean slate, the Kid continued to thieve and take more lives while riding with his band of renegades. The duty of running down the Kid was laid upon Pat Garrett. In the fall of 1880, Garrett was elected sheriff of Lincoln County and was eventually able to run down the Kid in the abandoned area of Stinking Springs. Surrounded and horseless, the Kid surrendered in April 1881. Held in Mesilla, he awaited his trial. Again, shocking the West, the Kid escaped, taking the life of one of Pat Garrett's deputies in doing so; again a loner, as he had always been in spirit. On July 13, 1881, Sherriff Garrett rode him down just outside of Fort Sumner. The Kid, barefoot, met his fate. The Kid lay dead, never speaking a word. At 21 years young, Billy lay with his many victims, mysterious even in death. The Kid was the most complex of young loner outlaws. He once told a newspaper "I wasn't a leader of a gang, I was for Billy all of the time!" For those who rode along side of the Kid, the few who knew him at all would say, "In his darkest of dangerous moods, his face always wore a smile. He ate, laughed, drank, laughed, rode, laughed, fought, then laughed; he would kill; then laugh."

BEEF/CHICKEN AND VEGETABLE KABOBS

When you BBQ the next time don't forget the kabobs! Great when you go camping or have a crowd over for a BBQ.

2 pounds boneless skinless chicken breasts or beef chunks cut into 1 inch cubes

2 cups Italian salad dressing

½ cup olive oil

1 teaspoon garlic salt

½ teaspoon salt

½ teaspoon fresh ground pepper

2 medium zucchini cut in ½ inch slices

2 yellow summer squash cut in ½ inch slices

2 medium onions, quartered

2 sweet red peppers, 1 inch pieces

3 cups cherry tomatoes

2 cups broccoli, cut into pieces

In a small plastic bag, combine chicken/beef and 1 cup of salad dressing. Coat meat and refrigerate 15 minutes. Coat veggies with oil, garlic salt, salt and pepper. Discard marinades. Fill 16 metal or soaked wooden skewers, alternating veggies and meat. Grill kabobs over medium heat until juices run clear from chicken and beef, turning and basting occasionally with remaining salad dressing.

PORK TENDERLOIN ROAST

Great recipe from Shana DeRoo. She tells us, "This is an easy and tasty method to cook a pork tenderloin. I start to cook my roast after lunch and dinner is ready when the family comes home from work and school."

1 whole pork tenderloin roast

1 large onion, peeled and sliced

1 whole garlic

Pepper, salt, and garlic powder

2 cups chicken broth or 2 cans of Swanson
    Chicken broth

Johnny's Seasoning, MSG free

Pre-heat oven to 300°. Place roast in deep roasting pan with fat side up. Stuff garlic cloves into roast (one every couple inches). Cover entire topside of roast with pepper, salt, and garlic powder. Place onion slices on top. Season over onions and roast with Johnny's Seasonings; add chicken broth around the meat base. Cover roaster and cook at 300° until roast reaches 155° to 160° internal temperature. Time will vary according to size of the roast. Be patient! Slowcooked equals tender meat! When done allow roast to sit for 10-15 minutes; juices will reabsorb back into meat. Place roast on serving platter, slice thinly and serve.

MEXICAN CHICKEN CHOWDER

A great soup for a cold evening. Recipe from my sister-in-law Corinne Abernathy.

3 chicken breasts

½ cup chopped onion

1 garlic clove, minced

3 tablespoons butter

2 chicken bouillon cubes

2 cups hot water

2 cups half and half

2 cups cheddar cheese, shredded

1 can (17 oz.) cream style corn

1 small can chopped green chilies

½ teaspoon black pepper

2 ripe tomatoes, chopped

Cut up chicken. Brown chicken, onion, and garlic in butter until chicken is done. Dissolve bouillon in hot water and add chicken. Pour into a large soup pan and simmer for a few minutes. Reduce heat. Add half and half, cheese, corn, chilies and pepper. Stir in tomato. Ready to serve.

The boots of early cowhands never had a right and a left —
just a pair of mule ear flaps on top to pull them up!

VENISON DELIGHT

Lots of venison at our home throughout the years. Always looking for tasty recipes. This is great!

About 2 pounds venison steak

1 cup onion, chopped

1 cup fresh mushrooms, chopped

1 beef bouillon cube in one cup water

1 teaspoon soy sauce

Salt and pepper to taste

1 cup sour cream

Cut venison steak into strips. Roll in flour and brown in butter. Remove meat and cook onions and mushrooms in butter until tender. Add meat, soy sauce, and beef bouillon. Salt and pepper to taste. Cover and simmer for an hour. Add sour cream. Serve over rice or potatoes.

MELT-IN-YOUR-MOUTH WAPITI

Heidi shares, "If I had a penny for every slice of this delicious steak over the years, Abe Lincoln would treat! There's a wide misconception about wild game tasting.. 'rank, gamey, tough, etc'. This is not true when cooked this way. We've had some of our service boys call from Iraq stating that this is what they want upon returning home! Just try it and you will believe it."

Slab of backstrap or tenderloin- Elk, Deer, or Moose

Flour   Salt and pepper   Cooking oil

Slice fresh or frozen meat very thin (¼ inch) against the grain into small steaks. Place slices on top of heavily floured large platter. Salt and pepper generously, dredge well! Fry in hot oil, turning each piece with spatula to keep "crust" on. Maximum cooking time: 5 minutes. Serve with homemade cheese hotcakes.

Dinners in those days were very plain. Game was stewed with vegetables in one great kettle – hotchpot this was called – a wonderful example of "one piece meals" that today's homemakers are so greatly interested in. Venison, pheasant, wild hare, squirrel, pigeons, plover from the marsh woods, and many kinds of fish formed the basis of this dish.

VENISON HINTS

1. Cook venison with low heat and treat like low quality beef.

2. Do not over-cook, for deer meat has short fibers that toughen quickly if over-cooked. Plan to serve venison medium well done.

3. Remove all venison fat before cooking. If fat is desired, add ground beef or pork or beef fat.

4. Venison is a dry meat, so add a moistener such as beef fat or cover surface with bacon strips.

In early times on the Oregon trail, a calf was required to fill half its stomach with milk, then butchered. The stomach was removed, washed, and hung to dry. Dried, it contained rennet, a substance used to curdle milk. This product was the first ingredient in making cheese.

In another time —
a gun, woodstove and pantry
made America.
— Andy Devine

GRANDMA'S CREAM BISCUITS

My grandma made everything with heavy cream, and her daughters, my aunts, followed her teachings. Good wholesome cooking.

5 cups flour

3 tablespoons sugar

1 tablespoon baking powder

1 teaspoon salt

½ cup cold butter

1 tablespoon yeast

2 tablespoons warm water

1 cup heavy cream

1 cup buttermilk

Mix dry ingredients in a bowl. Cut in butter as for pie crust. Dissolve yeast in warm water and add to cream and buttermilk. Add liquid ingredients to dry ingredients; mix well. Place dough on a lightly floured board and knead about 5-6 times. Roll out dough to ½ inch; cut into biscuits. Brush tops of biscuits with cream and a sprinkle of sugar. Let stand for 20 minutes. Bake at 400° for about 12-15 minutes or until golden brown.

STRAWBERRY BLACK PEPPER BUTTER

A special taste to spread on that fresh loaf of bread or fluffy biscuit.

3-4 fresh strawberries, finely chopped

¼ teaspoon fresh ground black pepper

½ cup butter, room temperature

Combine all ingredients. Mash gently with a fork until mixed. Chill until firm. Form into desired shape. Once the butter is chilled it is ready for lip-smacking bites.

In spite of many hazards and drawbacks to pioneer life, the loneliness and silence of the Plains were the very worst for the women to endure.

Ulysses S. Grant died of throat cancer. He smoked about 20 cigars per day for most of his life.

ZESTY GRILLED CHICKEN SALAD

This recipe is from Renee' Juntunen's kitchen.

SALAD:

1-2 grilled chicken breasts

2 Romaine lettuce hearts, chopped

1 cucumber, seeded and sliced

1 pint cherry tomatoes, cut in halves

¾ cup black olives

Salt and pepper

DRESSING:

1 ¼ cups feta cheese

3 tablespoons plain whole milk yogurt

1 teaspoon oregano

1 garlic clove

3 tablespoons red wine vinegar

6 tablespoons olive oil

½ red onion, sliced

Blend ½ cup feta cheese and all dressing ingredients together except for onion. After blended, stir onion into dressing mixture and let sit for 1 hour. Toss all salad ingredients with dressing mixture and remaining feta cheese before serving.

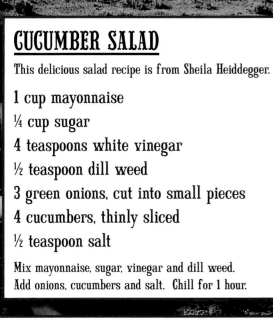

CUCUMBER SALAD

This delicious salad recipe is from Sheila Heiddegger.

1 cup mayonnaise

¼ cup sugar

4 teaspoons white vinegar

½ teaspoon dill weed

3 green onions, cut into small pieces

4 cucumbers, thinly sliced

½ teaspoon salt

Mix mayonnaise, sugar, vinegar and dill weed.
Add onions, cucumbers and salt. Chill for 1 hour.

"My son, you are now flesh of our flesh and bone of our bone. You are taken into the Shawnee."

– Blackfish, Shawnee

1778 adoption of Daniel Boone into the tribe.

CHILI RELLENO CASSEROLE

A very tasty good casserole from Em Miller.

4 (4oz.) cans mild whole green chilies

5 ½ cups grated Monterey Jack cheese

3 ½ cups grated sharp cheese

4 eggs

4 tablespoons milk

2 tablespoons flour

Pre-heat oven to 375. Lightly grease a 9x13 baking pan. Cut chilies into strips and remove seeds. Alternately layer chilies with cheese. Beat eggs, milk and flour together. Pour egg mixture over layered ingredients and bake for approximately 1 hour or until firm. Cut into squares and serve warm with salsa and green onions.

"COWBOY UP" BEANS

A great western twist on baked beans.

1-26 ounce can Bush's Original Baked Beans

1-26 ounce can Bush's BBQ Baked Beans

1-26 ounce can pork and beans, drained

1/3 cup brown sugar

1/2 cup ketchup

1 squirt mustard

1 package polish sausage, sliced

1/4 cup onion, chopped

1/3 cup green pepper, chopped

Combine first six ingredients in a casserole dish or crock pot and stir thoroughly. Brown sliced sausage with onion and pepper, then add to bean mixture. If cooking in crock pot, simmer on low until heated through. If using casserole dish, cook at 350° for 45 minutes in oven.

NEEDLEWORK OF YESTERDAY

Come and work with me through the needle's eye; the view is all encompassing.... See the weary mother's brow mending father's work worn shirt, the strong and loving hands creating exquisite stitches on her daughter's bridal gown.. glimpse the dwindling spool of thread that has to last all winter.

The dim lantern light strains the vision now as growing children clamor for clothes that fit...sewing – ahhh! The humble needle and thread represented security and warmth, works and intricate art, endless labor, social survival with dear friends: a woman's very sanity in early America.

Come and look with me through the needle's eye at your Great-grandmother's beautiful quilt... do you really see the sacrifice and the devotion imprinted there?

Hand sewing is an art form that is ancient. The first sewing needles were made of bones or animal horns and the first thread was made of animal sinew. Iron needles first appeared in the 15th century.

People had to invent weaving, spinning and other techniques and machines needed in order to make the fabrics used for clothing. Before sewing machines, nearly all clothing was local and hand sewn. There were tailors and seamstresses in most towns that could make individual items of clothing for customers. After the sewing machine was invented, the ready-made clothing industry took off.

The first functional sewing machine was invented by the French tailor, Barthelelmy Thimonnier, in 1830. Thimonnier's machine used only one thread and a hooked needle that made the same chain stitch used with embroidery. The inventor was almost killed by an enraged group of French tailors who burnt down his garment factory because they feared unemployment as a result of his new invention.

Sewing machines did not go into mass production until the 1850's, when Isaac Singer built the first commercially-successful machine. Singer built the first sewing machine where the needle moved up and down rather than from side to side and the needle was powered by a foot treadle. Previous machines were all hand cranked.

THE BEST BREAD IN THE WEST

A fine-grained delicious bread recipe from Candy Wallace. She tells us to use hard white wheat flour or if you grind the wheat yourself she prefers Golden 86 hard white wheat.

2 cups boiling water

1 cup rolled oats, uncooked

Pour boiling water over oats. Let stand until thoroughly softened.

^{2}/$_3$ cup warm water

1 tablespoon salt

½ cup honey

2 tablespoons oil or butter

Add water, salt, honey, and oil/butter to the oats. Add:

2-3 cups whole wheat flour

1 tablespoon yeast

2-3 more cups whole wheat flour

Knead for 5 minutes. Let rise 1 hour. Cover with a damp cloth. Makes 2 loaves. Place in two greased bread pans. Brush tops with honey and sprinkle with dry oats. Let rise for 30 minutes. Bake at 350° for 35 minutes.

ZUCCHINI BREAD

A lowfat good quick bread recipe from Candy Wallace.

1 ½ cups flour

½ teaspoon baking soda

½ teaspoon baking powder

1 teaspoon cinnamon

¼ teaspoon nutmeg

1 cup sugar

1 cup zucchini, shredded

¼ cup oil

1 egg

¼ teaspoon lemon peel, grated

½ cup walnuts, chopped (optional)

Combine all dry ingredients in bowl. Mix together. Add zucchini, oil, egg, and lemon peel. Mix all ingredients together and bake at 350° for approximately 60 minutes. Makes one loaf.

WESTERN RANCH SALAD

Let the sunshine in with this crisp salad. With fresh corn off the cob, this salad will receive rave reviews.

4 cups mixed lettuce, torn

1 (15 oz.) can black beans,
   rinsed and drained

2 cups fresh corn, cut off the cob

1 sweet red pepper, chopped

2 small green onions, chopped (optional)

2 cups fresh tomatoes, chopped

1 cup cheddar cheese, grated

Put lettuce in a flat, round bowl. Top with beans, corn, peppers, tomatoes and lastly cheese. Drizzle with ranch dressing and sprinkle with cracked pepper.

POPCORN DELIGHT

Recipe from Cheri Mattson.

²/₃ cup white popcorn
¼ cup oil
⅛ cup parmesan cheese
Garlic salt

In a 6 quart sauce pan, put in oil and popcorn. Cook on high temp till oil is bubbling and popcorn starts to pop. Turn down to medium heat and shake kettle over burner till popping stops. Dump popped corn immediately into bowl and sprinkle with cheese and desired amount of garlic salt (not too salty). Stir up with two forks and enjoy! So delicious...your company will want more!

BAKED CORN

This recipe is a little different from the one in The Old Farmhouse Kitchen cookbook. It is great!

1 egg
2- 12 ounce cans, whole kernel corn, drained
1 cup evaporated milk
¾ cup shredded Swiss cheese
2 tablespoons chopped onion
½ teaspoon salt
¼ teaspoon pepper

Beat eggs; stir in corn, milk, cheese, onion, salt, and pepper. Pour into baking pan. Sprinkle with topping; bake at 350° for 45 minutes.

TOPPING:

½ cup bread crumbs
2 tablespoons butter, melted
¼ cup Swiss cheese, melted

HORSESHOE SANDWICH

A Western recipe for sure from Debbie Amundson. Her mother-in-law, Bev, says, "This sandwich is delicious." We agree!

Frozen French fries (or make your own)
Cheese sauce (recipe follows)
8 slices toasted white bread (I use sourdough)
8 baked ham slices or cooked beef patties
Dash of ground paprika

Prepare frozen French fries per package instructions. Prepare cheese sauce. To assemble sandwich: Place 2 slices of toasted bread side by side on individual serving platters; top with either ham slices or cooked beef patties. Cover with cheese sauce, and mound a large amount of French fries on top and along the sides. To garnish, sprinkle with paprika. Serve immediately. Makes 4 servings.

CHEESE SAUCE

3 egg yolks

1 cup veggie or chicken broth

4 tablespoons butter

6 cups shredded sharp cheddar cheese

2 teaspoons Worcestershire sauce

½ teaspoon dry mustard

No salt

1 teaspoon black pepper

1 teaspoon cayenne pepper

Optional:

Debbie tells us "I also make a basic white sauce with ¼ cup butter, ¼ cup flour, and 2 cups milk. Then lots of cheese after sauce is thick. Flavor with salt and pepper."

History of Horseshoe Sandwich

This sandwich is considered the signature dish of Springfield, Illinois, the home of Abraham Lincoln.

The original horseshoe sandwich was served on a sizzling metal plate (known as the anvil). Two thick-cut slices of bread were toasted and added to the plate. Then a thick slice of ham, shaped like a horseshoe, was added, to it a Welsh rarebit cheese sauce made of white sharp cheddar, and then just before serving, fresh-made French fries were added as the (nails) in the horseshoe. The secret to this sandwich is the delicious cheese sauce. Today's sandwiches now offer either a thick fried ham slice or two large hamburger patties, and the cheese sauce is poured over the fries. The name of the sandwich comes from the shape of the ham with the fries representing the horseshoe nails, and the heated steak platter is the anvil. If you order a pony shoe sandwich, it is the same thing, but a smaller or half a horseshoe portion (usually one slice of toast).

STRAWBERRY SHORTCAKE

This is a melt-in-your-mouth delightful shortcake for those beautiful strawberries. The cornmeal is a wonderful addition. Try it!

1 ¾ cups flour

¼ cup cornmeal

6 tablespoons cold butter, cut in small pieces

1 ½ teaspoons baking powder

½ teaspoon salt

1 tablespoon sugar

1 egg, beaten

²/₃ cup whipping cream

1 tablespoon butter, melted

2 teaspoons sugar

Add cold butter to dry ingredients and mix with a pastry blender. Whisk together egg and cream; add to flour mixture, stirring just until dough forms. Knead a couple times. Transfer dough to lightly floured board. Pat dough into a six-inch circle. Cut in six wedges; gently separate wedges by at least one inch and place on greased baking sheet. Brush tops with melted butter.

Sprinkle with sugar. Bake at 400° for about 20 minutes until golden. Cool and top with sweetened strawberries. Serve with whipped cream or ice cream.

MOLLY'S BROWNIES

For a large group you can't beat this good recipe for chocolate brownies. The secret is not to over bake them. Recipe from Molly Kangas.

1 ¼ cups butter	1 ¼ cups baking cocoa
4 cups sugar	1 teaspoon salt
8 eggs	2 teaspoons vanilla
2 cups flour	2 cups nuts, chopped

Cream butter and sugar together. Add one egg at a time and beat well. Mix in sifted dry ingredients. Add vanilla and nuts. Spread batter on a greased, 10x15 inch baking pan. Bake at 350° for 35-40 minutes.

FROSTING:

½ cup butter	3 cups powdered sugar
1 ½ squares, unsweetened or white chocolate	5 teaspoons milk
	1 teaspoon vanilla

Melt butter and chocolate, add milk, powdered sugar, and vanilla. Spread on warm brownies.

I wear moccasins laced to my knee, dress in layered smoke-soaked skins and carry a long-barreled Kentucky rifle. I'm a Texan, rounding up rebel steers. A cow-hunter I am called, the first western cowboy!

This Steelhead was caught on the east fork of the Lewis River. My grandson Jason Gillette and Owen Kysar traded me the fish for pancakes, bacon, and eggs!

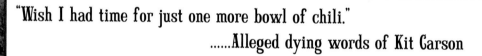

"Wish I had time for just one more bowl of chili."

......Alleged dying words of Kit Carson

Jump on the wagon train! Ride in the ruts that remain as scars, deeply embedded in the earth. Open your heart; invite the pioneer to dwell. Close your eyes; look at the beautiful, haunting truth as it was; yet as a vapor in the wind, it disappears, leaving us to reflect in wonder.....

BIG AND BOLD CHILI BEANS

This Yacolt Mountain chili is an absolute family favorite. It is wonderfully satisfying – make it and love it! From the Esteb Kitchen.

1 large yellow onion

2 pounds moose hamburger (beef can be used)

½ pound pork sausage

3 tablespoons olive oil

½ teaspoon garlic salt

1 pound red beans soaked overnight OR

6 - 15oz. cans small red beans or beans of choice

1 - 6oz. can tomato paste

3 - 14oz. cans tomato sauce

2 - 14oz. cans sliced and stewed tomatoes

4 cups water

1 tablespoon chili powder

½ teaspoon cayenne pepper flakes

Fry first 5 ingredients on medium high, leaving meat chunks coarse. Stir frequently; brown very well. Add meat mixture and rest of ingredients to large stock kettle. Simmer on medium-low on stove top, stirring often, for 45 minutes. You may also put in large crock pot on low heat for 4-5 hours. Serve in large bowls with sour cream on top.

POTATO FLAT BREAD

Extremely easy and fragrant – melts in your mouth. Recipe from Heidi.

Stir together, until dissolved:

3 tablespoons yeast

2 cups warm water

¾ cup sugar

Mix together and add to above:

2 cups half and half scalded 3 minutes in microwave

1 cup mashed potatoes OR quality dried potato flakes

Add:

2 beaten eggs (She uses one nice big duck egg and one nice chicken egg)

Place in large bowl, add yeast mixture and whisk.

Stir in:

6 cups flour (your favorite)

3 teaspoons salt

Dough will be soft; dump on floured work surface. Knead 3-4 minutes, working in ¾ cup flour. Cut into 3 equal hunks. Generously grease 2 large cookie sheets. Using heel of hand, hammer each one into flat oval. Prick with fork. Melt ½ cup butter; pour over loaves. Generously sprinkle Parmesan cheese over top. Let rise one hour, bake at 375˚ until crust is very brown, 30-40 minutes.

PONY EXPRESS

The Pony Express galloped across our country for the first time on April 3, 1860. Hard driven riders and hundreds of horses were pounded to exhaustion, as this fast paced mail-carrying system delivered news across the continent. (This was a five month journey). The pony express cantered to a stop only 19 months after it started! By 1876, vast spaces came closer together as the new telegraph lines opened up a fresh, uncharted communication highway in the sky.

HEIDI'S SPECTACULAR SPAGHETTI

1 large onion, chopped

2 pounds moose hamburger or ground beef

½ pound pork sausage (optional)

3 tablespoons olive oil

1 - 6oz. can tomato paste

2 - 14oz. cans tomato sauce

2 - 14 oz. cans stewed tomatoes

1 tablespoon chili powder

1 teaspoon Italian seasoning

1 teaspoon garlic salt

1 teaspoon fresh ground pepper

2 cups grated sharp cheddar cheese

Fry first 4 ingredients (medium-high), stirring frequently. Brown very well. Add rest of ingredients. Simmer on low 10-15 minutes. Remove and pour over cooked, drained, and rinsed spaghetti. You may use any type of noodle for a different look: bow tie, penne, macaroni or thin spaghetti. Stir well, spread in a 9x13 pan. Spread 2 cups sharp cheddar cheese over all. Bake for 20 minutes on 375°. Serve bubbling hot with good French bread and you will make an instant friend!

DREAMY ALFREDO SAUCE

This is a must-have recipe from Sarah Tapani.

½ cup butter

½ cup heavy whipping cream

¾ cup parmesan cheese, grated

½ teaspoon salt

Dash of pepper

⅛ teaspoon garlic, minced

Heat butter and whipping cream in saucepan over low heat stirring constantly until butter is melted. Stir in the rest of ingredients until cheese is melted and sauce is heated through. Can either be served over 8 ounces of cooked fettuccine noodles or used as a dipping sauce for pieces of crusty bread or breadsticks.

BRAN MUFFINS

A great way to start your morning, and the fiber is very good for your health. Recipe from Mary Sneeden.

2 ¼ cups wheat bran

1 cup whole wheat flour

1 teaspoon baking powder

1 teaspoon baking soda

½ cup molasses

½ cup honey

½ cup milk

½ cup oil or applesauce

2 eggs

Mix and bake in greased muffin tins for 20-25 minutes at 350˚.

BROTHELS

Brothels and bathhouses were a shameful subject in the Old West, highly disapproved of by the settlers. But alas! The love of money ruled this ancient profession, and monstrous amounts of money were made! This was a constant battle for the righteous and upstanding citizens who felt so strongly against these drinking, carousing facilities. The long debates and heated arguments never ended. On October 10, 1879, the editor of the Leadville Daily Chronicle wrote, "men are fools and women are devils in disguise."

STEAK

Grill that steak outside on the grill or make a campfire. Nothing compares with the taste. Salt and pepper with a few hot peppers is fantastic.

A Cowboy's Hat

My hat's on my home
My home is my head
My saddle's my pillow
The ground is my bed

My hat's my trademark!
I'm this and I'm that...
But a cowboy's nothing
Without his hat!

Good judgment comes from experience... and experience – well, that comes from poor judgment.

RANCH HOUSE STEAK

Who doesn't enjoy a good steak, especially if it is flavorful and tender? Fee Fie Foe Yum, I smell a fantastic steak.

2-3 1-inch New York or Rib-Eye steaks
3 tablespoons butter
4 tablespoons apple juice or orange juice
1 medium onion, sliced and grilled
1 tablespoon Dijon-style mustard
Salt and pepper to taste

Heat butter in a skillet. Brown meat on both sides. Remove meat and keep warm; add juice, grilled onions, and mustard to skillet; cook and stir until blended. Return steaks to skillet and cook for 2-4 minutes on each side to the doneness you like. Serve.

Solitary Trees,
If they grow at
all, grow strong
-Winston Churchill

ALL-AMERICAN APPLE PIE

All-time favorite by popular demand since the 1600's. Pick the right apples if you want a prize pie. Gravenstein apples are the best. I freeze these apples for pie in the winter.

Make pastry for a two crust pie.

Mix together:

6 cups peeled and sliced tart apples

¼ cup flour   **2 tablespoons butter**

1 cup sugar   **Cinnamon**

Heap apple mixture in pastry-lined pan. Sprinkle with cinnamon and dot with 2 tablespoons butter. Cover with top crust and seal edges. Sprinkle with sugar. Bake at 375° for about 45 minutes or until fork tender and crust is golden. Serve with cream or ice cream and always have slices of cheddar cheese available.

ROOT CELLARS

Root cellars have been used since the 18th century to store turnips, carrots, parsnips, cabbage, potatoes, and other crops through the cold winter months. These crops were used for human consumption but more importantly to feed dairy cows, beef cattle, and sheep. The vegetables provided critical vitamins and other nutrition necessary to keep up milk production, fatten cattle, and improve the live birth rate of sheep in the early spring. By the mid-1800's, root cellars became a means to store crops destined for the markets until mid-winter or later when much higher prices could be commanded. Root cellars became largely obsolete with the introduction of modern refrigeration and switch to feeding livestock with corn and other grains along with silage stored in silos. In the past decade there has become renewed interest in root cellars.

This is my husband Sonny's homeplace, built around 1937.

CRANBERRY ALMOND MUFFINS

Long before the first frontiersman came to America, Indians harvested wild cranberries for food and medicine. The pilgrims thought the berries' pink blossoms resembled the heads of wild cranes. They named the fruit "crane" berries. Later the name was changed to cranberries. Tart cranberries are oh so good with almonds in the muffins.

1 ¾ cups flour

½ cup whole wheat flour

¾ cup brown sugar

1 tablespoon baking powder

½ teaspoon baking soda

½ teaspoon salt

½ teaspoon cinnamon

1 cup cranberries, cut in half or, coarsely chopped

¾ cup almonds, chopped

¼ cup melted butter

1 cup half and half

1 egg, beaten

Combine dry ingredients. Mix butter, half and half, and beaten egg together and add to flour mixture, stirring just until moistened. Divide batter among 12 muffin cups. Bake at 400° for about 20 minutes.

It was 1903 when Pearl Zane Grey, an un-
distinguished New York dentist, sat writing
Western literature in a dingy room between
patients. By 1924, his books began to
sell. Although to some, Grey's writings
seemed overloaded with lengthy descriptions,
the American readers as a whole fell in
love with his works. The main difference in Zane Grey stories compared to all
other western writers of that time is
the romance he wove into all of his
books. He placed charming women and
a sweet love story in his settings,
intriguing several generations of young
Americans. The Riders of the Purple Sage
are still galloping through my heart, remind-
ing me of the innocence of my youth.

PEANUT BUTTER COOKIES

Judy and Gerald Tikka kept me nourished with these very good cookies at an auction. Judy got the recipe from Anna McDaniels Lehman.

Cream all together:

1 cup butter

1 cup white sugar

1 cup brown sugar

1 cup peanut butter

½ cup buttermilk

1 teaspoon vanilla

2 teaspoons baking soda in 1 tablespoon warm water

3 ½ cups flour

½ teaspoon salt

Drop on greased cookie sheets, flatten with fork. Bake at 400° for 8-10 minutes

MARBLES

Some of the oldest recorded rules for marble games were in a book published in 1866 called PLAYGROUND. The game of marbles is played with variations from playground to playground all around the world. Good clean fun.

The basic game of marbles is a simple one. The first decision to make is whether you are playing for "keepsies" (where the winner gets to keep your marbles if you lose) or just for fun.

The game begins by knuckling down at the edge of a circle at least 3 feet around and each player flicks their shooter until all the marbles are hit. Remember, the shooter marble must not leave the circle.

A favorite of most all of us older ones! We had fun playing the game and now we collect marbles!

DISHPAN DONUTS

One of Pete Kysar's many surprises are his doughnuts. Years
ago he'd decide to make doughnuts and boy did he make 'em.
"Wasn't any use having doughnuts unless you could fill a dish pan full.
Chester Abernathy would eat them with me. He would get real happy
to see my dish pan full of doughnuts instead of dishes," Pete tells us.
Pete used a big ol' black cast iron pan "and genuine pig lard in and out"
to cook these delicious doughnuts. This recipe is out of Pete's wife Ruth's
1938 Household Searchlight cookbook.

BLEND CAREFULLY:

1 cup sugar

2 eggs, beaten

SIFT TOGETHER:

4 ¾ cups flour

1 teaspoon salt

3 teaspoons baking powder

½ teaspoon cinnamon

½ teaspoon nutmeg

⅛ teaspoon ginger

ADD ALTERNATELY WITH FIRST MIXTURE AND FLOUR MIXTURE:

1 cup milk

2 tablespoons melted shortening

½ teaspoon vanilla

½ teaspoon lemon flavoring

Chill dough. Turn onto lightly floured board and roll in sheet ⅓
inch thick. Cut with floured cutter. Fry in deep fat at 365°
until brown. Drain on crumpled absorbent paper. Sprinkle with sugar.

This old recipe was written in the 1930s by the hand of Marie Koschnitzki Lynch Johnson (1888-1964) on a telegram paper from the Yacolt Telephone Office. It was operated by Julia Garner Worthington, whose family names live on through two local rural roads. Marie's granddaughter, Carolyn Rinta, says the sugar is to be browned in a skillet.

PACIFIC TELEGRAM

THE PACIFIC TELEPHONE AND TELEGRAPH CO.

THE PACIFIC TELEPHONE AND TELEGRAF CO.

CLASS OF SERVICE

| TELEGRAM | | DAY LETTER | SYMBOL DAY L. | NIGHT MESSAGE | SYMBOL NITE | NIGHT LETTER | SYMBOL N.L. |

IF NONE OF THE THREE SYMBOLS SHOWN ABOVE APPEARS AFTER THE CHECK (NUMBER OF WORDS) THIS IS A TELEGRAM. OTHERWISE ITS CHARACTER IS INDICATED BY THE SYMBOL APPEARING AFTER THE CHECK.

RECEIVED AT

Burnt Leather Cake

1½ cups sugar
1   "   butter
3 teaspoon carmel = 1 teaspoon mollass
2   "   Vanilla
3   "   Baking powder
2½ cups flour
3 eggs
1 cup water
   "   Sour cream filling

½ cup sour cream
1½ "   sugar   Boil till soft ball beat till thick

Photo of Marie K. L. Johnson taken in 1940 near the front porch of Rinta's Farmhouse in Yacolt, Washington.

TIMELESS CUSTARD PIE

One of my father's favorite pies, an old time dessert.

1 large pie shell
2 cups milk, warmed
½ cup half and half, warmed
4 eggs, slightly beaten

½ cup sugar
1 teaspoon flour
½ teaspoon salt
1 teaspoon vanilla
cinnamon/nutmeg to your taste

Roll out pie crust to fit a 9-10 inch pie plate. Shape and crimp edges. Refrigerate. Mix together dry ingredients in a bowl. Stir in eggs and vanilla. Gradually add warmed milk and half and half; mix well. Pour custard into chilled pie shell. Sprinkle cinnamon/nutmeg on top of pie. Bake at 400° for 35-40 minutes or until an inserted knife comes out almost clean. Chill pie before serving.

GRANDMA'S COCONUT COOKIES

Bonnie Gilligan from University Place in Washington sends us this recipe along with the following message. "When I was a little girl, my mother worked at the Del Monte Cannery in Vancouver during the summer. While she worked, I got to stay with my grandma. Since she lived on a farm, there were lots of fun things to do but my favorite thing was making cookies. Making cookies is therapeutic for me so my freezer is always stocked with several dozen cookies ready to be used or shared as needed. When my mom made cookies, they were small – no more than two bites. When Grandma made cookies, they were big – like a meal in themselves. No wonder I liked Grandma's cookies best. My grandma made the best cookies and my favorite cookies were her coconut cookies. I'd like to share the recipe with you."

½ cup white sugar

½ cup brown sugar

½ cup shortening

1 egg

1 cup flour

1 teaspoon baking powder

1 teaspoon baking soda

1 teaspoon salt

1 cup rolled oats

1 cup coconut

Cream sugars and shortening. Add egg. Mix well and add dry ingredients. Add rolled oats and coconut. Drop from a spoon onto greased cooking sheet. Bake at 350˚ for 10 minutes. Yield: 3 dozen. The cookie dough is dry so don't get discouraged when mixing up a batch – it does all come together. It's best to double this recipe because these cookies are so good! These used to be my brother Stan's favorite cookies; he liked nuts in the batches and batches I made.

SUNSHINE WATER

This drink brings a surprised smile to everyone. Cheri claims it's like sunshine in your mouth. So thirst quenching and refreshing! Serve on a hot summer day, or with chips and salsa.

1 gallon water

2 cups sugar

7 fresh squeezed lemons

2 apples, chopped in ¼ inch squares

(Cantaloupe pieces chopped small may also be added)

Refrigerate and serve!

SWEET TEA

Our daughter Cheri has made sweet tea for years. I prefer some fresh lemon added.

4 cups water

8 tea bags (Lipton black tea)

½ cup honey or sugar

4 cups cold water

Bring 4 cups water to a boil, add tea bags. Boil 1 minute; remove from stove. Cover and steep 10-15 minutes. Remove and discard tea bags. Stir in honey or sugar. Pour into pitcher, stir in 4 cups of cold water. Pour over ice in glasses.

RICHARD'S FIBER BARS

I gave Richard and Patricia Peldo some of my seed bars and Richard decided to make his own recipe with the seeds ground and chopped. Completely different, but ever so tasty and good.

1 cup flaxseed, ground

1 cup pumpkin seed, ground

2 cups almonds, finely chopped

1 ½ cups pecans, finely chopped

1 ½ cups walnuts, finely chopped

1 cup carob chips

1 ¼ cups butter

4 cups marshmallows

Mix all together, heat on top of stove until marshmallows and butter are melted. Pour out into a 9x13 pan. Cut into bars.

CRUNCHY SEED BARS

Everyone wants this recipe and for some reason it goes unnoticed in "The Old Farmhouse Kitchen" cookbook. I often get asked for this healthy fiber bar.

1- 16 ounce bag marshmallows

½ cup butter

2 cups flax seeds

1 cup sesame seeds

2 cups pumpkin seeds

1 cup sunflower seeds

1 cup coconut

2 cups almonds, roasted

1 cup pecans, roasted

You can use seeds, dried fruit, and nuts of choice. Melt butter and marshmallows in a large bowl in microwave. When melted, add seeds, nuts and coconut. Pour into 9x13 buttered pan. Cut into 1x3 inch bars.

EGGS IN BREAD HOLLOWS

Over the campfire or in your kitchen, these eggs are good.

Sourdough bread, cut into thick slices
Oil or butter
Eggs

Cut the bread into thick slices. Make a circle and remove it from the center of the bread. Fry the bread on both sides until golden. Drop an egg in the hollowed-out center of the bread. Turn down the heat and cook until egg is done. Season with salt and pepper.

CANNING FRUIT SYRUP:

1 cup sugar to 1 cup water makes a very rich syrup.

2 cups sugar to 3 cups water makes a rich syrup.

1 cup sugar to 2 cups water makes a thinner syrup.

For jams and jellies, follow the recipe on the pectin box. I like to cook some of my preserves for a couple hours, using less sugar. I pour the jam into hot sterile jars, apply hot lids and screw down the rings tightly. Music to your ears is the sound of the lid sealing.

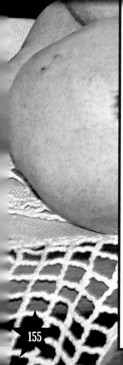

RASPBERRY PEAR COBBLER

In the West we have an abundance of fruit. This is a quick recipe and you can use your frozen raspberries.

2 cups frozen raspberries, thawed

⅓ cup sugar

3 teaspoons cornstarch

3 cups fresh pears, peeled and sliced

TOPPING:

1 cup flour

½ cup sugar

½ teaspoon salt

1 teaspoon baking powder

1 egg, beaten

¾ cup sour cream

2 tablespoons butter, melted

Drain raspberries; save syrup. Add enough water to syrup to make 1 ¼ cups. In saucepan, combine 1/3 cup sugar, cornstarch, and syrup. Cook and stir until boiling well. Add raspberries and pears. Pour into nine-inch square pan. Combine flour, ½ cup sugar, baking powder and salt. Mix egg, sour cream and butter; add to flour mixture; mix well. Drop dough by spoonfuls onto thickened fruit. Bake at 350 for 30 minutes.

PEAR BUTTER

Peel and remove insides with the seeds and stringy pulp. To quartered pear halves, add a little water in the roasting pan. Cook in the oven at 325° until the pears thicken. Sugar to taste and add desired amounts of cinnamon, allspice, and nutmeg. It will take at least three hours. So good at Christmas in little tarts.

Home-Dried Fruits and Vegetables

Long before canning, refrigeration, and freezing, foods were dried to preserve them. Dried foods were eaten when fresh foods were unavailable. Now, many of us take these lightweight packages of dried morsels backpacking and camping, especially in the fall for hunting trips. Naturally air dried or mechanically dehydrated, foods free from moisture keep well.

The Basics for Canning and Preserving

I want to impress upon everyone, do not mix time tables of various types of canning and preserving. Learn any one type well and stick to that. If you use a pressure cooker, stick to the required time. Do not attempt to process in water from a pressure cooker time table.

You cannot improve qualities by canning. You can only get out of a jar what you put into it. A sound and fresh product, well canned, will give you a tasty, wholesome food. It is so satisfying to open the jam, jellies and fruits you have labored in the summertime to can and preserve. If you get brave and use the pressure cooker directions, you will have a meal from your jars!

The main advice you get from me is quite simple: always get everything ready before filling.

1. Wash jars, rinse and sterilize in hot water before filling. A dishwasher works. It is best if jars are warm when you fill them.

2. Pack food mixture into warm jars, leaving a good inch of head room. Jams only need ½ inch space between food and lid. Pour the prepared syrup over fruit.

3. Wipe top of jar off, apply hot lids and screw on lids.

4. Put filled jars into warm water in the canner. Water should cover jars at least an inch. Turn on heat. Watch for a boil.

5. When water starts boiling, follow process time directed in the recipe. I time quart jars of apricots, peaches, and pears for 20 minutes after they start boiling. I always lower the heat so the water is boiling but not too hard. Berries do NOT require the full 20 minutes.

6. Remove jars using a jar lifter when processing time is completed. Cool on rack.

HOMEMADE SAUERKRAUT

This recipe is from Julie Scherbarth. Her grandmother Germaine Rotschy Russell gave her this recipe. Julie says it is her favorite sauerkraut method. Harvest those beautiful cabbages for a fun experiment.

40 pounds shredded cabbage
1 pound salt

Layer cabbage and salt, in a very large bowl. Mix well until cabbage is starting to sweat or make juice. Pack into sterile, clean, wide-mouthed jars. Pack the cabbage down firmly until ½ inch from the top of jar. Wipe off rims and place cap and ring on, tighten. Line a large wash tub with newspaper and set quarts in the tub. Cover with a large towel and keep tub with cabbage in a warm to mild place. Jars will bubble and stew for approximately 4-5 days. Don't panic! This is okay! Jars will start smelling like sauerkraut as they work. When fermentation stops, wash off jars, rinse seals and lids; wipe lids. If needed add some water to bring liquid up to the neck of the jar, about 1 inch from top. Replace dry lids and seals. Process in boiling water bath for 15 minutes. Ready to eat in 4-6 weeks. Yummy!

Only after the last tree has been cut down, only after the last river has been poisoned, only after the last fish has been caught, only then will you find money cannot be eaten.

— Cree Prophecy

COWBOY

A Haiku format assignment at Yacolt School.

Draw from the hip, shoot gun
Strong punch and kick with tough boot
Buckskin torn to threads
By: Grandson Jeffry Gillette

Horace
Durfey on Circle C

'40

Horace Durfey: 90 years old. A true blue old time cowboy. In 1938, at 13, Horace left home searching for work. He found it harvesting peas for 35 cents an hour. Following his dream to buckaroo, he went on to be Buckaroo Boss, working on thousands of acres of range land, shipping tens of thousands of steers at a time to market. When World War II started, Horace signed on to break horses for the 2nd Cavalry of the U.S. Army. He loved breaking the fine thoroughbreds for our country.

"Two of us would work as a team with a string of about ten horses at a time. When they were inspected and approved by the colonels, we'd take on another string. We'd get a lot of good ones and a lot of bad ones in the Cavalry. Mean ones we'd call cougars, they'd kick, scrap and bite."

The mannerly cowboy remembers, "I made $150.00 a month. Boy! That was good money then. 43,000 head of thoroughbreds were in the Cavalry. Old Army officers thought they were gonna win the war with the Cavalry. Us younger ones knew they had planes and stuff. After the war they didn't know where all the horses should go, so they butchered, canned, and fed the poor with them. Those were hungry times for people. Back then, the hide was always torn off my hand from breakin' those broncs...It hardly ever healed up." When asked the total count of horses he's broken in his lifetime, Horace just smiled modestly and replied, "Well, I did it for forty years...at three to ten at a time, how many can you remember?" He went on to say that the worst injuries he got were on the gentlest horses. "I got to trusting too much. You had to be ready to get back on and ride!" Horace is one of, or maybe the only remaining WWII Cavalry horsemen of the US Army. This honorable cowboy shares his very favorite meal: Buckaroo Spuds.

"We used to take and chop up and cook a bunch of bacon. Not crisp. Spill the grease off of it. Cut potatoes and onions in an old cast iron frying pan. Fill up with water. Let cook and cook. When water boils down, taters get soft. It gets a little thick. They start smellin' good too! You always have bacon, onions and potatoes around buckaroo camps!"

STEAK FAJITAS

A real favorite at Gabrielle and Joe's house. And, they are easy to make; so flavorful.

2-3 pounds round steak

1 clove garlic

2 teaspoons salt

½ teaspoon black pepper

1 teaspoon oregano

2 tablespoons olive oil

1 cup lemon or lime juice

12 corn or flour tortillas

1 cup sour cream

1 ½ cups shredded lettuce

3 ripe tomatoes, chopped

Salsa

Cut steak into strips 6 inches long. Mash garlic and seasonings together; add olive oil and coat meat with seasonings and olive oil. Place single layers of steak in a glass baking dish. Pour lemon or lime juice over steak and marinate at least 30 minutes. Grill steak over coals or fry. Cut steak pieces into smaller pieces. Roll up in tortillas; add sour cream and salsa. You can use guacamole also. We like the lettuce and tomatoes.

COCONUT BERRY-PEACH PIZZA

A wonderful quick summer treat for picnics or even for breakfast company.

2 (8 oz.) tubes crescent rolls

1 (8 oz.) package cream cheese, softened

1 cup powdered sugar

2 tablespoons berry jam

2 cups whipping cream, whipped

3 fresh peaches, sliced

1 ½ cups fresh strawberries, sliced

2 cups fresh raspberries

1 cup blueberries or blackberries

1 cup flaked coconut, toasted

Unroll crescent roll dough and place in a greased 15x10 inch baking pan. I use the pans we buy from Costco. Seal crescent roll seams. Bake at 375˚ for 15-20 minutes or until golden brown.
Cool on wire rack. Whip cream, set aside. Beat cream cheese, sugar, and jam until smooth. Fold into whipped cream. Spread over cooled crust. Arrange fruit over the top. Sprinkle with coconut and chill.

BLITZ KUCHEN

This is a yummy easy recipe from Greta Nudd. It tastes a lot like snickerdoodle cookies.

¼ cup shortening

1 cup sugar

2 eggs

½ cup milk

1 ½ cups flour

1 teaspoon baking powder

1 teaspoon vanilla

Mix all together and put into a 9x13 pan. Mix cinnamon and sugar and sprinkle on top. Bake at 350˚ for 25-30 minutes.

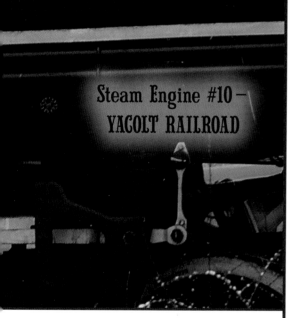

Steam Engine #10 –
YACOLT RAILROAD

SETT WESTERN CO.

THE RAILROAD

In 1864, when President Abraham Lincoln approved the building of the rail line, a massive, feverish construction took place. Chinese coolies and Irish laborers rhythmically drove spikes into the ties on the Central Pacific and Union Pacific railroads. Within three years, these rolling, rumbling tracks joined the two great oceans. The railroad instilled a huge sense of excitement and enterprise. As with any change, it brought some frowns, but the astronomical impact of greatness and progress soon overrode any opposition! To this day, the sound of the train brings a delightful, childlike smile to the romantic at heart.

FUDGE

This unbeatable fudge does not have to be beaten! So easy, so creamy! So rich! Tastes heavenly! JoAnn Cummings gave us some fudge one Christmas years ago and I knew I had to have the recipe. Try it!

4 ½ cups sugar

1 (12oz.) can canned milk

⅓ cup butter

2 (8.4oz.) Hershey's chocolate bars, broken

1 (12oz.) package chocolate chips

1 (8oz.) jar marshmallow topping

1 cup chopped nuts (we like 2 cups)

Bring sugar, milk, and butter to boil in saucepan; boil for 5 minutes, stirring often. Remove from heat and quickly stir in remaining ingredients. Stir well; pour into buttered 9x13 pan. It makes about five pounds of fudge.

"GO WEST YOUNG MAN, GO WEST AND GROW UP WITH THE COUNTRY."

When Horace Greeley said this well-known quote, he actually meant to go no further west than Erie County, Pennsylvania! Beginning his career in politics as a Whig, Greeley helped establish the "new" Republican party in 1856. He helped Abraham Lincoln in decisions on the benefit and welfare of our America. Greeley urged the new generation to go west stating, "If you have no family or friends to aid you... turn your face to the Great West, and there build up your home and fortune."

SCOTCH SHORTBREAD

Sandra Easterly's yummy recipe!

½ pound butter, salted and soft

⅓ cup sugar

2 cups flour

Use a meat fork to stir; with larger chunks use the warmth of your hand to mix in the butter. Dump out onto a bread board or marble slab. Pat to desired thickness, approximately ¼ inch. Form into a rectangle on baking sheet. Cut into squares and prick each piece several times with a fork. Bake at 325° for 20 minutes or until light brown.

KNOX BLOX

Very colorful and decorative. Can be cut with cookie cutters of your choice. Children love these interesting blox!

4 envelopes Knox unflavored gelatin
3 (3 ounce) pkgs. flavored gelatin
4 cups boiling water

In a large bowl, mix all gelatin with boiling water, stirring until dissolved. Pour in a 9x13 baking pan; chill until firm. To serve, cut in 1 inch squares. Makes: 9 dozen blocks.

BERRY SUMMER SMOOTHIE

A true delight and easy to make.

1 cup berries, your choice	½ cup milk
1 frozen banana	pinch of salt
1 cup vanilla ice cream	½ cup 7-up

1 tablespoon frozen orange juice concentrate

In a blender, combine berries, banana, ice cream, orange juice, milk, and salt. Puree until smooth. Add 7-up and puree for 2 seconds. Serve immediately. Serves 2 people.

I ONCE HAD A DOLL

My Mother Lucy's sweet voice sang this song to me when I was a little girl. The dolly I hugged looked just like this one.

I once had a sweet little doll dears,
the prettiest doll in the world,
her cheeks were so red and so white dears,
and her hair was so charmingly curled.
But I lost my poor little doll dears
as I played on the heath one day.
I searched for over a week dears,
but I never could find where she lay.
Oh, I found my poor little doll dears
as I played in the woods one day.
Folks say she is terribly changed dears
for her paint is all washed away.
With her arms trodden off by the cow dears,
and her hair not the least bit curled,
yet for old sake's sake she is still dears,
the prettiest doll in the world.

— Charles Kingsley

172

APPLE TART

This recipe is from Rachel Rose. It is easy to make and Rachel put it in the oven to bake while we were eating supper. How delicious when so fresh and warm for dessert.

1 unbaked pie crust

4 ounces softened cream cheese

1 tablespoon powdered sugar

4 cups sliced apples

¼ cup sugar

2 tablespoons flour

1 teaspoon cinnamon sugar

Line 9 inch pie plate with crust. Spread cream cheese mixed with powdered sugar in a 6-inch circle in the center of crust. Toss apples with sugar and flour; spoon over cream cheese in center of pie plate. Fold crust partially over apples. Sprinkle with cinnamon sugar. Bake at 425° about 25 minutes; cover with foil the last 5 minutes. Serve warm with ice cream.

BAKED WHOLE-APPLE CRISP

An old-fashioned wholesome dessert and so easy to make ahead of time. Bake just before serving. We've baked apples for years.

8 baking apples

1 cup orange juice, divided

1 cup oatmeal

½ cup brown sugar

½ cup chopped almonds

1 tablespoon flour

1 teaspoon cinnamon

⅓ cup butter, melted

Core apples leaving a little on the bottom so crisp will stay inside apple. Place apples in a 9x13 pan. Brush apples with ½ cup orange juice. Combine oats, brown sugar, almonds, flour and cinnamon. Stir in melted butter. Fill and top apples with oatmeal mixture. When ready to bake, brush apples with the remaining juice. Cover with foil. Bake at 350° for about 45 minutes. Remove foil and continue baking for 15 minutes. Cool. Drizzle with honey and top with a spoon of whipping cream or ice cream.

ANIMAL CRACKERS

Children are wild about these little boxes of animal shaped cookies that have sold around America since 1902. Shirley Temple sang "Animal crackers in my soup." Even Webster's Dictionary acknowledges "animal crackers" as part of American life.

CHEERIOS NUGGETS

Recipe from my neighbor Merle Moore brings you back in time. Merle says she got her recipe from a friend's mother about 30 years ago.

In a greased 4 quart bowl, combine:

6 cups Cheerios

1 cup salted Spanish peanuts

1 cup raisins

In a 2 quart saucepan, combine:

1 cup brown sugar, packed

½ cup butter, softened

¼ cup light corn syrup

½ teaspoon salt

½ teaspoon baking soda, set aside

Preheat oven to 250°. Grease 2 rectangular pans 13x9x2", or 1 jelly roll pan 15 ½ x 10 ½ x 1". Heat the brown sugar, butter, corn syrup, and salt over medium heat, stirring constantly until bubbly around the edges. Cook uncovered, stirring occasionally, two minutes longer. Remove from heat, stir in baking soda until foamy and light brown in color. Pour over the cereal, peanuts and raisins mixture. Stir until mixture is coated. Spread evenly in pan (or pans) and bake 15 minutes. Stir and let stand just until cool, about 10 minutes. Loosen mixture with a metal spatula. Let stand until firm, about 30 minutes.

Shadows linger as
a coyote's lonesome howling
echoes to the moon.
— Andy Devine

COWBOY BREAD

This recipe is from Ima Massie. Ima says that she got this recipe in 1969 from a neighbor who cooked at the local school. She serves this good bread with chili.

3 cups flour

½ teaspoon salt

2 cups brown sugar

²/₃ cup butter

Mix well and take out one cup.

Add to flour mixture:

½ teaspoon baking soda

1 teaspoon cinnamon

1 teaspoon nutmeg, optional

1 cup buttermilk

2 eggs

Pour dough into a greased 9x13 pan and sprinkle reserved 1 cup of dry mixture over the top. Bake at 350° for about 30 minutes.

BUTTER COOKIES

This is our favorite rolled-out sugar cookie. This cookie can stay in a cookie tin for 2 weeks if stored in a cool place. JoAnn Cummings has made hundreds of these melt-in-your-mouth cookies for everyone. I try to make them at least twice a year because of special requests from our sons.

1 cup soft butter

½ cup sugar

1 egg

3 teaspoons flavoring (vanilla, lemon, almond, etc)

3 cups sifted flour

½ teaspoon baking powder

Cream butter, sugar, and egg; stir in flavoring. Sift together flour and baking powder and add to creamed mixture. Chill dough. Roll very thin, cut into desired shapes. Place on ungreased baking sheet. Bake at 400° for 7-9 minutes, cool and frost.

BUTTER ICING:

3 cups powdered sugar

½ cup melted butter

2 tablespoons milk

1 teaspoon vanilla

⅛ teaspoon salt

Sift sugar, combine with melted butter, vanilla, salt, and milk. Beat until creamy.

BONNIE AND CLYDE

Bonnie and Clyde!
Learned how to slide,
Through the long-reaching hand of the law –
Danger! And Romance
Was their dance...
It was sung to the tune of awe!

Robbing stores and banks,
Pulling sadistic pranks,
Shooting hundreds of bullets – was he!
A misplaced ambition,
Carrying a keen intuition,
Firing right beside him – came she!

They were crazy insane,
Lead riddled like rain
When Bonnie and Clyde were near –
Then justice of the land
Made a stand
In spite of terror and fear!

Setting a snare
With a wild hare
They waited for hours, seven-long
A large car's whine
Through the Louisiana Pine
Delivered them to the right – the wrong!

"Stick em' up", lawmen cried
As their fire opened wide
Oh! A massacre of bloodshed and gore!
A slow motion dream!
A panther-like scream,
Bonnie attempted to even the score!

Jerking his 10-gauge around,
Clyde tried blocking the sound
But alas, for him in vain
Silence became heard,
Dust muffled each word
Now the outlaws, unblinking...remain.

Betwixt the two
Remained a heart tattoo,
Rounds of ammo, and victims, and strife.
History was made,
As each body was laid
To its final departure from life!

COWBOY SUGAR COOKIES

Cheri tasted these delicious delights at her Montana friend Linda Walsten's house and begged me to put them in this book. The cookie sounds crunchy, but it is most definitely not! They melt in your mouth and you want another....and another!

CREAM TOGETHER:

1 cup butter	1 cup white sugar
1 cup oil	2 eggs
1 cup powdered sugar	1 teaspoon vanilla

ADD:

1 teaspoon cream of tartar	1 teaspoon salt
1 teaspoon baking soda	4 ½ cups flour

Roll into tablespoon sized balls (on the larger side). Stamp down with bottom of glass that has been greased and dipped in sugar. Bake 10 minutes at 350˚. Cheri uses fork to press down cookie with ½ teaspoon sugar for a pretty top! Stamp cookie to approximately ½ inch thick (no thinner). She also adds cinnamon to sugar for a quick snickerdoodle.

Oh the memories of dear Dr. Clark! He had his office in Battle Ground. In the days when we had no telephone, Dad would drive to Amboy, about five miles, to call Dr. Clark. About four hours later here he came with his huge hypodermic needle and a large vial of penicillin. Each of us got our portion in the buttock, and let me tell you, it really hurt! Being young I can't remember if he changed the needle, but obviously it didn't matter. Dr. Clark was so kind and nice and he loved to visit with our daddy. He usually went to our cousins nearby and caught the Kysars on the way back to Battle Ground. That was the end of the epidemic until the next time. I still wish I had the old coffee grinder Dad traded him on one of those many doctor calls. We were blessed to have such an accommodating doctor available.

CRANBERRY PUDDING

We were fortunate to visit with Dr. Calvin Clark and his wife, Arlene at a supper invitation at Dr. Robert Rose and his wife, Rachel's home. Arlene was happy to share this cranberry pudding recipe. Calvin's father was our hero doctor many years ago. Arlene reports that through the years, Mother Clark gave all the grandchildren a steamer and a copy of this recipe. It is a Clark family tradition. The only year that was unique, was the one when she added charms to the pudding, the finders to be brought good luck. When someone almost lost a tooth as they bit into one, it was decided to never do that again- no matter how much good luck the charms were supposed to bring!

¼ cup brown sugar	½ teaspoon salt
¼ cup molasses	1 ½ cups flour and 2 teaspoons baking soda mixed together
½ cup hot water	2 cups cranberries, each cranberry cut in half

Mix together. Lightly grease the steamer pot, sprinkle the greased inside with granulated sugar, pour in pudding, and then place it into a large kettle with a lid to steam for 2 hours. Then remove the steamer pot and let this cool a little. Invert the steamer and gently let the formed pudding emerge. If using immediately, top with sauce and light the sugar cube. If using later, wrap the cooled pudding in saran wrap or foil, store in the refrigerator until used. Before serving, warm the pudding in the oven at 200˚.

SAUCE:

1 cup sugar	½ cup cream (we use half and half)
½ cup butter	1 teaspoon vanilla

Bring to a boil. Spoon over pudding. Top with a sugar cube soaked in lemon extract. When everyone has their serving, the cubes are lighted and everyone in the family sings "We wish you a merry Christmas!", reports Arlene.

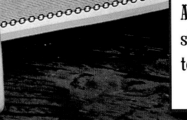

A doctor's hand bag stocked with necessities- to cure the feeble.
– Andy Devine

WINTER COFFEE

Melt chocolate in boiling water. Add sugar, salt, milk and cream, vanilla, and coffee. Whip with fork until foamy. You are in for a chuck wagon surprise.

1 ounce square unsweetened chocolate

2 cups boiling water

¼ cup sugar

Dash of salt

1 cup milk and cream, mixed

1 teaspoon vanilla

2 cups hot coffee

HOT CHOCOLATE MIX

Many of us have made this hot chocolate for years. I got the recipe from Leila Kysar. This recipe makes 1 gallon of mix.

8 quart package powdered milk

1 pound box Nestle's Quik

6 ounce jar Coffee-mate

2 cups powdered sugar

Mix together. Use approximately ¼ cup of mixture to 1 cup boiling water.

Darci Frazier presents us with this wonderful recipe. She says: "When those first snowflakes fall, my boys beg for this treat." It brings back so many memories to me. When I was a child we didn't have many treats, times were tough and pieces of candy were far and few between. In the winter time we always had snow ice cream! This recipe makes 1 quart.

SNOW ICE CREAM

2 eggs
½ cup sugar
1 cup milk or light cream
2 teaspoons vanilla
Pinch of salt

Place ingredients in a large bowl. Beat with an egg beater and this will make an *uncooked custard. Now, scoop up a pan of new fallen snow and mix the snow into the custard. You'll need to eat this right away! So delicious!
*If frightened of salmonella the custard can be cooked and cooled when it first starts to snow.

LEMON MERINGUE CAKE

We all agree, this cake gets a blue ribbon. We all love lemon pie and this is close to the taste. This is an easy way to make cake.

3 cups cake flour

1 tablespoon baking powder

½ teaspoon salt

¼ teaspoon baking soda

1 ½ cups butter, softened

1 ¼ cups sugar

⅔ cup milk

2 teaspoons vanilla

4 large eggs

Mix together dry ingredients. Set aside. Cream together butter and sugar until fluffy. Beat in flour mixture, milk, vanilla and eggs until well blended. Batter should be fluffy. Grease and flour three 9-inch cake pans. Spread batter evenly into prepared pans. Bake at 350˚ about 20 minutes or until a toothpick inserted into the center comes out clean. Cool slightly and put the cakes to cool on a rack. When cake is cool slice through each of the three cakes carefully. Spread cooled lemon filling on all the layers and in between layers.

LEMON FILLING:

Mix in saucepan: 1 ½ cups sugar   ⅓ cup cornstarch   1 ½ cups water
Cook over medium heat, stirring constantly, until mixture thickens and boils. Boil 1 minute. Slowly stir at least half the hot mixture into 3 egg yolks, slightly beaten. Then blend into hot mixture in saucepan. Boil 1 minute longer, stirring constantly. Remove from heat and blend in 3 tablespoons butter and ½ cup fresh lemon juice, with a little grated lemon rind.

MERINGUE:

1 cup egg whites   1 cup sugar

Make meringue by whisking egg whites and sugar together. Set over a pan of simmering water until mixture is warm and sugar is dissolved. Beat on high speed until light and fluffy, about 2 minutes. Place cake on a bread board and frost with meringue. Broil until golden brown. Serve on a pedestal plate.

He Loves Me...
He Loves Me Not...

BLACKBERRY TREAT

When I was a child and then in the first years of marriage, we waited for the little wild blackberries to ripen. The berries grow on old logs and around in the woods. It takes quite a while to pick a quart of these divine "hard to fill your pail" blackberries.

2 quarts wild blackberries (you can also use marionberries or boysenberries)

1 cup sugar

3 tablespoons cornstarch

Boil and thicken berries. Place your favorite crust pieces on top of bowls when serving with cream or ice cream.

NEVER FAIL PIE CRUST

This recipe is a grand winner! If you cannot seem to make a flaky pie crust, now you can, using this recipe!

3 cups flour
1 teaspoon salt
1 ½ cups shortening
1 beaten egg
1 tablespoon vinegar
4 tablespoons cold water

Cut shortening into flour and salt until the mixture is the size of small peas. Add water, vinegar, and beaten egg. Roll out dough and cut into shapes with a cookie cutter. Bake on a cookie sheet until golden brown around the edges. Bake at 400° for about 13-15 minutes. Remove from pan and cool. You can also use dough for a double crust pie of your choice.

RHUBARB CUSTARD PIE

Julie Russell Scherbarth tells us: "I have a rhubarb custard pie recipe that was Grandma Germaine Rotschy Russell's that I'd like to share with you. Like her, I never measure a lot of things so I hope it turns out for you. It has a great custard center to it and is so good!"

4-6 cups chopped fresh rhubarb

¼ teaspoon lemon zest

4 tablespoons flour

4 large fresh eggs, right out of the hen house!

2 teaspoons cinnamon, optional

Grated nutmeg, just a little, optional

Sugar to taste, maybe 1 -1½ cups

Pie crust for pie pan, bottom and top crust

In a large bowl, place chopped rhubarb and flour and mix together until rhubarb is coated. In another bowl mix together sugar, eggs, zest, and spices. Mix well, then pour over rhubarb and mix all together. Pour into pie shell and cover with second crust. Vent the top with a design. Brush milk on top and sprinkle sugar over top of crust. Bake at 375°-400° for 40-50 min.

BANANA CREAM PIE

1 baked pie shell
1 cup milk
1 cup half and half
1 tablespoon cornstarch
2 tablespoons flour
½ cup sugar
½ teaspoon salt
2 eggs, beaten
1 teaspoon vanilla

Heat milk and half and half in microwave carefully until boiling. Combine cornstarch, flour, sugar, and salt. Mix together thoroughly. Using a whisk or egg beater, add to hot milk. Bring to boil, stirring often. Spoon some of the hot mixture into beaten eggs, a little at a time. Pour together and bring to a light boil. Stir in vanilla. Cool with wax paper on top to keep a thicken-ed layer from forming. When cool, add sliced bananas and pour into cooled pie shell.

Time will slow a bit —
for those who on their journey
stop and smell the rose.

— Andy Devine

MOM'S ANGEL FOOD CAKE

Recipe from Debbie Rinta. Debbie tells us, "We used to have chickens when I was a kid. Thus we had lots of eggs to use up. Mom made angel food cake quite often. I can still see the big Pyrex mixing bowl, the beaters I loved to lick and the cake cooled upside down on an old Pepsi bottle. Forty-some years later mom still uses that same pop bottle! One difference with her cake was the square pan she used- everyone else's was round. I still prefer the square!

MEASURE AND SIFT TOGETHER:

1 cup Soft as Silk cake flour

1 cup granulated sugar

MEASURE INTO A LARGE BOWL:

1 ½ cups egg whites (approximately 12 eggs)

1 ½ teaspoon cream of tarter

¼ teaspoon salt

Beat until foamy with electric mixer or wire whip. Add a scant ¾ cup sugar a little at a time. Continue beating until mixture forms stiff peaks.

FOLD IN:

1 ½ teaspoon vanilla

½ teaspoon almond flavoring

Sift the flour and sugar mixture ¼ cup at a time, over the meringue and gently fold in with a rubber spatula. Repeat until all the flour and sugar mixture has disappeared (dissolved). Push batter into 10x4 tube pan. Use knife to gently cut through the batter to remove large air bubbles. Bake at 375˚ until top springs back when lightly touched, about 30-35 minutes. Invert on a funnel or glass pop bottle after baking to cool. Hang until cold. Frost with 7-minute frosting or strawberry powdered sugar frosting as follows.

BLEND:

⅓ cup soft butter

3 cups powdered sugar

4-5 tablespoons crushed strawberries

• Also good with fresh strawberries and REAL whipped cream! (A Mother's Day special for our family!) If I'm feeling lazy or hurried, I've been known to buy (gasp!) angel food cake and tear it into bite size pieces and layer it in a clear glass bowl with pudding/cool whip and fresh fruit.

VANILLA CUSTARD ICE CREAM

1 ¾ cup granulated sugar
¼ cup brown sugar
6 tablespoons flour
1 teaspoon salt
5 cups milk

6 eggs, beaten
1 cup half and half
2 cups heavy cream
2 tablespoons vanilla

Combine sugars, flour and salt. Add beaten eggs and milk. Cook and stir over low heat until thick. Do not boil. Remove from heat. Stir in half and half and cream. Cool. Add vanilla and pour into 4 quart freezer. Place dasher in the ice cream freezer can. Put lid on can and place can in bucket. You're ready to go!

"I scream, you scream, we all scream for ice cream!" What would our summers have been without luscious homemade ice cream? The rich custard was always made ahead so it would cool. Remember, we had the old-time refrigerators with a block of ice to keep our food cool. The ice cream freezer container was packed into the wooden freezer bucket with crushed ice and rock salt, and cranked by all present until even the strongest could barely turn the handle. Then out came the dasher, covered with soft, sweet ice cream and we all got a dripping spoonful before the freezer was packed in heavy blankets to let the ice cream ripen. Electric machines have replaced the hand-crank variety at our home. We have four freezers for large gatherings. Now we pack the ice cream in newspaper and put it in the freezer for an hour. The taste is still the same!

ICE CREAM

Recipe from Debbie Rinta. Her grandpa Jewell made this using Butterfingers.

1 quart heavy whipping cream
1 quart half and half
2 tablespoons vanilla
1 ½ cups sugar
¼ teaspoon salt

Mix and freeze. (Follow your machine's directions.) Approximately 3 Quarts- We like to add crunched up Butterfinger candy bars, fresh fruit, or crunched Oreos or ....possibilities.

PEANUT BUTTER AND
CHOCOLATE CHIP COOKIES

Recipe from Debbie Rinta. Excellent!

2 cans (14 oz.) sweetened condensed milk
1 ¼ cup creamy peanut butter

Mix until smooth.

Add:

4 cups graham cracker crumbs, finely crunched

Stir. Then add:

12 oz. semi sweet chocolate chips

Mix well. Drop by teaspoonfuls onto ungreased cookie sheet and bake at 350˚ for 12-14 minutes until light brown.

KILLER COLESLAW

A very tasty coleslaw from Tom and Heidi.

1 ½ pounds shredded cabbage
1 teaspoon salt
²/₃ cup sugar
⅓ cup vinegar
1 cup whipping cream

Shred cabbage and chill for 1 hour. Mix the rest of ingredients and pour over chilled cabbage. Stir well before serving, sprinkle with powdered sugar in serving bowl.

TOM'S TUM TUM SALMON

A great recipe from my son-in-law, Tom Esteb.
Tom says "Sweet treat that's loved by all". I agree.

- Place fillets in a pan or aluminum foil boat, skin down.
- Sprinkle heavily with brown sugar.
- Salt fish.
- Sprinkle light amount of lemon pepper and dot with 1 cup butter per pound of fish.
- Bake at 350° for 40 minutes or until flaky.
- Remove and cool for 15 minutes; serve.

TOM'S KIPPERED FISH

A delicious fish. Enjoy with cheese and crackers.
You can use salmon, steelhead, or trout. Recipe from our son-in-law, Tom.

- Cut fish into fillets or steaks.
- Sprinkle with brown sugar and salt.
- Smoke for 1-2 hours with heavy smoke.
- Place fish in pint jars and add ½ teaspoon salt to each jar.
- Follow directions in your pressure cooker book.
- Cook at 10 pounds pressure for up to 90 minutes.

Gun-slinging outlaws of the Old West —
Butch Cassidy and the Sundance Kid formed the gang known
as the **WILD BUNCH**. They were responsible for the most
successful train and bank robberies in American history.

COCONUT CAKE

Very moist and delicious, from Sally Tapani. Tanya Abernathy uses vanilla instant pudding
between layers.

2 cups sugar

4 eggs

2 ½ cups flour

½ teaspoon salt

1 tablespoon baking powder

1 cup oil

1 cup unsweetened coconut milk

1 teaspoon vanilla

1 teaspoon almond extract

Beat eggs and sugar; add rest of ingredients. Bake at 350° for 30 minutes in two 9-inch
pans, cool and frost.

FROSTING:

Blend well

½ cup butter

4 ounces cream cheese

3 cups powdered sugar

¼ cup unsweetened coconut milk

½ teaspoon vanilla

½ teaspoon almond extract

Slice each cooled layer in half. Put filling/frosting in between, then frost entire cake.
May garnish frosted cake with flaked coconut.

HOMEMADE MAYONNAISE

Homemade is always the best! If cowboys wanted mayonnaise, the camp cook whipped it up. A recipe worth making from Charlayne Kolshinski.

⅓ cup flour

1 teaspoon sugar

1 teaspoon salt

1 teaspoon dry mustard

¾ cup water

¼ cup mild vinegar or lemon juice

4 egg yolks (or 2 whole eggs)

1 cup salad oil

Mix flour, sugar, salt, and mustard in a saucepan. Gradually add water and vinegar. Cook over low heat, stirring constantly until mixture boils. Boil one minute. Remove from heat. Pour into bowl. Beat in egg yolks with rotary beater. Continue beating, adding salad oil a little at a time. Chill before serving. Makes 2 cups.

MAYONNAISE CAKE

A good moist cake. Try it, you'll enjoy the goodness. From Charlayne Kolshinski.

1 cup dates, chopped

1 cup walnuts

1 teaspoon salt

1 teaspoon baking soda

1 cup hot water

While above ingredients are soaking, prepare mixture below:

1 cup mayonnaise

1 cup sugar

2 cups flour

2 tablespoons cocoa, unsweetened

1 teaspoon vanilla

Mix all together with dates and walnut mixture. Bake at 350˚ for 40-50 minutes in 9x9 greased pan.

HAZELNUT COOKIES

These cookies are quite nutritious and very tasty! Recipe from Lori Anne Homola.

1 ½ cups peanut butter

½ cup butter

½ cup brown sugar

1 cup white sugar

2 teaspoons vanilla

3 eggs

2 teaspoons baking soda

½ cup flour

4 cups oatmeal

1 cup butterscotch chips

1 cup chocolate chips

1 ½ cups roasted and chopped hazelnuts

Heat oven to 350°. Cream together peanut butter, butter, brown sugar, white sugar, vanilla and eggs. Add flour, oatmeal, and soda. Stir in chocolate chips, butterscotch chips and nuts. Drop by spoonfuls on cookie sheet. Bake 12-14 minutes. Cool 2 minutes before removing from cookie sheets.

I will lift up mine eyes unto the hills, from whence cometh my help. My help cometh from the Lord, which made heaven and earth.

Psalm 121:1,2

CHOCOLATE RICE KRISPY TREATS

A true treat without turning on your oven- no baking!
Recipe from Lori Anne Homola.

4 tablespoons butter

1 (14oz.) package marshmallows

6-8 cups Rice Krispies

¾ cup chocolate chips

1 ½ cups roasted almonds

In a large bowl, melt butter, chocolate chips, and marshmallows in microwave. Heat only 2 minutes at a time, stirring in between until marshmallows and chocolate are melted. Add Rice Krispies and almonds and mix well. Pour into buttered 9x13-inch pan and pat down. Cool and cut into squares.

FRUIT CAKE

I make this wonderful fruit cake every Christmas. It is Leila Kysar's recipe with some changes.

CREAM TOGETHER:

1 cup butter

2 cups brown sugar

BEAT IN:

5 eggs

1 teaspoon vanilla

ADD ALTERNATELY:

½ cup milk

½ cup strawberry jam

WITH:

2 ½ cups flour

1 teaspoon baking powder

1 teaspoon salt

1 teaspoon cinnamon

MIX TOGETHER WITH ½ CUP FLOUR AND ADD TO OTHER INGREDIENTS:

1 pound dates

3 cups candied cherries

1 cup candied pineapple

3 cups dried fruit, chopped

2 cups walnuts

2 cups pecans

2 cups almonds

2 cups Brazil nuts

Bake 1 ½ hours at 300˚ in greased and paper lined loaf pans. *I put candied cherries and pecans on top of fruitcake before baking. If you spoon Karo Syrup on top, the cherries and nuts will stick on the cake.

PEACH COBBLER

When peaches are fresh and ripe be sure to make this sweet yummy recipe. It is hard to stop eating at one bowl.

1 ½ cups flour

2 tablespoons brown sugar

2 teaspoons baking powder

½ teaspoon salt

6 tablespoons butter

¾ cup whipping cream

6 cups peaches, sliced

2 tablespoons cornstarch

1 cup granulated sugar

Cut cold butter into dry ingredients using a pastry blender until mixture is like coarse meal. Stir in whipping cream. Put peaches, cornstarch, and sugar into a baking dish. Stir and mix. Roll out dough to ¼ inch thickness. Cut out 1 ½ to 2 inch rounds and place on top of peaches. Brush tops of dough with cream and sprinkle with sugar. Bake at 350° for 35-40 minutes or until golden brown. Fruit should be bubbling. Serve warm with ice cream or cream.

WALNUT FUDGE COOKIES

These cookies are chewy, nutty and surprisingly low in fat. Nancy Massie is a pro at making these very good cookies. She always adds chocolate chips.

Set oven to 400° degrees. Cut parchment paper or brown paper bag to fit cookie sheet. Combine in large mixing bowl:

4 cups powdered sugar

7 egg whites

1 cup unsweetened cocoa

½ teaspoon vanilla

3 cups walnuts

¼ teaspoon salt

Mix slowly for about 2 minutes making sure all ingredients are thoroughly incorporated (the mixture should look soupy). Bake immediately; do not let batter stand! Line baking sheet with paper. Drop by tablespoonfuls onto the paper leaving at least 1 inch in between each cookie. Bake for 10 to 12 minutes. Remove immediately by pulling the paper and the cookies on to the wire rack to cool. Use fresh paper for each batch. Note: these cookies dry out quickly. When cool, place in Ziploc bags to store.

BAKER CHOCOLATE'S BIRTH

In 1764 America's sweet tooth was found. Twelve years before the signing of the Declaration of Independence and before America had a president, a small industry was making chocolate under the brand name Baker's. Who could have realized how satisfying America's favorite taste would become?

COCOA
AND
CHOCOLATE

WALTER BAKER & CO. LTD
DORCHESTER, MASS.
ESTABLISHED 1780.

BILLY BOY

Oh, where have you been,
Billy Boy, Billy Boy?
Oh where have you been,
Charming Billy?
I have been to seek a wife,
She's the idol of my life.
She's a young thing,
And cannot leave her mother.

Did she bid you to come in,
Billy Boy, Billy Boy?
Did she bid you to come in,
Charming Billy?
Yes, she bade me to come in,
And to kiss her on the chin.
She's a young thing,
And cannot leave her mother.

Can she bake a cherry pie,
Billy Boy, Billy Boy?
Can she bake a cherry pie, Charming Billy?
She can bake a cherry pie,
Quick's a cat can wink her eye.
She's a young thing,
And cannot leave her mother.

How old may she be,
Billy Boy, Billy Boy?
How old may she be,
Charming Billy?
Three times six and four times seven,
Twenty eight and eleven,
She's a young thing,
And cannot leave her mother.

Can she bake a cherry pie,
Billy Boy, Billy Boy?
Can she bake a cherry pie,
Charming Billy?
She can bake a cherry pie,
Quick's a cat can wink her eye.
She's a young thing,
And cannot leave her mother.

Written by: author unknown

CHERRY PIE

A favorite dessert. Serve with ice cream.

2 crusts for a nine inch pie
1 cup sugar
4 tablespoons cornstarch
3 cans tart cherries
1 teaspoon almond extract
2 tablespoons butter

Pre-heat oven to 400˚. Drain cherries and reserve juice from two of the cans. Pour juice into a sauce pan along with cornstarch and sugar. Cook over medium heat, stirring constantly until mixture thickens. Remove from heat and add cherries and almond extract. Pour filling into pastry lined pie plate. Dot with chunks of butter. Put on top crust; seal and vent. Bake 30-40 minutes until crust browns and filling is bubbling. Cool pie before slicing.

While cheerfully making this pie you can sing about Billy Boy.

When burying dead loved ones along the wagon trail, wailing mourners left the shallow graves, knowing animals and grave robbers would come behind, unearthing the bodies. Exposed bones lay bleaching along the rolling plains. Human skulls inscribed with personal messages stamped frightening images in the traveling pioneer's brain; yet even more horrifying was how soon they grew accustomed to the unforgettable sights.

The Lord is my shepherd; I shall not want.

Psalm 23:1

WILLIE KEIL GRAVE

On the hill behind is the grave of Willie Keil, nineteen year old son of Dr. William Keil, leader of the Bethel Colony that came west to settle here in November 1855. Willie was to have driven the leading team in the wagon train which was to leave Bethel Missouri in May 1855. Four days before their departure, Willie died. Because of his great desire to go west with the group, the decision was made to take his body along. It was placed in a lead-lined box filled with alcohol. The sealed coffin was carried in a wagon remodeled as a hearse which led the wagon train west. In the evening by lamp-light, Willie was buried here November 26, 1855.

– taken from tombstone in Eastern Oregon

BREAKFAST

EGGS AND SPUDS, COWBOY 25
EGGS IN BREAD HOLLOWS 154
FARINA MUSH, ENRICHED 5
FLAPJACKS, OVERNIGHT BUCKWHEAT 10
FRENCH TOAST, SWEET BREAKFAST 2
HASHBROWNS, SPICED 1
OATMEAL CEREAL, OLD-FASHIONED 5
OATMEAL CEREAL, HEARTY STEEL CUT 22
OMELET, WESTERN 7
PANCAKES, CORNMEAL 17
PANCAKES, WORKING MAN CHEESE 2
PIZZA, BREAKFAST 16
PIZZA CRUST 16
PRUNE-SAUCE, LUMBERJACK 17
PUDDING, HASTY 6
SAUSAGE, HOMEMADE 17

BREADS

BREAD . . . .
   BROCCOLI CORN 21
   BROWN 89
   COWBOY 178
   INDIAN FRY 38
   NO FAIL WHITE 41
   NO KNEAD 35
   POTATO FLAT 134
   PUMPKIN 8
   SADDLE BAG PULL APART 105
   SOURDOUGH STARTER 13
   SOURDOUGH 13
   THE BEST IN THE WEST 124
   ZUCCHINI 124
BUNS . . . .
   BUFFALO BURGER 54
   CORNMEAL 33

BISCUITS . . . .
   CHEDDAR 87
   CORNSTICKS, INDIAN 38
   DONUTS, DISHPAN 147
   GRANDMA'S CREAM 116
   SWEET APPLE CINNAMON 27
MUFFINS . . . .
   BRAN 136
   CORN 64
   CRANBERRY ALMOND 143
ROLLS . . . .
   CARAMEL PECAN 45
   SWEET POTATO 44

MAIN DISH

ALFREDO SAUCE, DREAMY 135
BACON, SWEET PEPPERED 15
BEANS . . . .
   BBQ BAKED 77
   COWBOY UP 122
   MOMMY'S BAKED 28
   NAVY BEANS AND HAM 88
   SALAD, HOT BEAN 77
BUFFALO BURGER 54
CHICKEN, FRIED 66
CHILI . . . .
   BIG AND BOLD BEANS 134
   BRIAN'S LEAN MEAN 91
   BUFFALO 89
CHILI RELLENO CASSEROLE 121
CABBAGE, PAN FRIED 82
CLAMS, OLD TIME FRIED 94
CORN, BAKED 126
ENCHILADAS, CHICKEN 92
FAJITAS, STEAK 163
FISH, TOM'S KIPPERED 196
GRAVY, RED 99
HASH, WESTERN 84

HOMINY FOR COWPOKES. 61
KABOBS, VEGGIE, CHICKEN AND BEEF 109
NACHOS, BUCKAROO. 104
PARSNIPS, CANDIED 81
PORK CHOPS, SWEET AND SOUR OLD WEST . . . 58
PORK, SIDE 15
POTATOES, CHEESY MASHED 99
PUDDING, SWEET CORN BREAD 101
RABBIT, FRIED 52
RIB, PRIME 71
RIB ROAST, PRIME 71
ROAST BEEF, LONG HORN 83
ROAST, PORK TENDERLOIN 110
SANDWICH, HORSESHOE. 127
SAUERKRAUT, HOMEMADE 159
SALMON CASSEROLE 68
SALMON, PLANKED. 20
SALMON, TOM'S TUM TUM 195
SHRIMP BOIL 94
SPAGHETTI, HEIDI'S SPECTACULAR. 135
SQUASH, WINTER 82
STEAK, RANCH HOUSE. 140
TONGUE, TASTY 60
TRI TIP, BBQ. 31
VEGETABLES, INDIAN ROASTED 57
VENISON DELIGHT. 113
WAPITI, MELT IN YOUR MOUTH 113
ZUCCHINI, FRIED 31

TOMATO, WESTERN MARINATED 57
STEWS . . . .
   APPLE CIDER 37
   CABBAGE PATCH 100
   COWPUNCHER 63
SOUPS. . . . .
   CHOWDER, MEXICAN CHICKEN 111

COOKIES AND BARS

BARS. . . . .
   BROWNIES, MOLLY'S. 131
   CRUNCHY SEED. 153
   FIBER, RICHARD'S. 153
   KUCHEN, BLITZ 165
   RICE KRISPIE TREATS, CHOCOLATE 202
COOKIES . . . .
   BUTTER 179
   COCONUT, GRANDMA'S 150
   FUDGE, WALNUT 205
   HAZELNUT 201
   MAPLE 106
   PEANUT BUTTER 145
   PEANUT BUTTER AND CHOCOLATE CHIP . . 194
   SHORTBREAD, SCOTCH 170
   SUGAR, COWBOY 181

SALADS, SOUPS, AND STEWS

SALADS. . . . .
   CHICKEN, ZESTY GRILLED 119
   COLESLAW, KILLER 195
   CUCUMBER. 120
   LEMON DILL 66
   RANCH, WESTERN 125

PIES AND CRUSTS

PIES . . . .
   APPLE, ALL AMERICAN 141
   BANANA CREAM 190
   CHERRY PIE 206
   CUSTARD, RHUBARB 189
   CUSTARD, TIMELESS 149
   HUCKLEBERRY 40
   SWEET POTATO/SQUASH 43

CRUSTS . . . .

    NEVER FAIL 188

    OLD WEST 56

DESSERTS

APPLE TART 173

BLACKBERRY TREAT 187

COBBLER, PEACH 204

COBBLER, RASPBERRY PEAR 155

CRISP, BAKED WHOLE APPLE 174

DONUTS, DISHPAN 147

FUDGE. 168

ICE CREAM. 194

ICE CREAM, SNOW 184

ICE CREAM, VANILLA CUSTARD 193

KNOX BLOX 171

PECAN ROLLS, CARAMEL. 45

PUDDING, BREAD 50

PUDDING, CRANBERRY 182

PUDDING, RICE. 49

PIZZA, COCONUT BERRY PEACH 165

SHORTCAKE, STRAWBERRY 129

CAKES

ANGEL FOOD, MOM'S 192

COCONUT 198

COFFEE, APPLE. 12

FRUIT 203

GERMAN CHOCOLATE 73

LEMON MERINGUE 186

MAYONNAISE 199

BEVERAGES

COFFEE BOILED, OUT ON THE RANGE 3

COFFEE, WINTER 183

HOT CHOCOLATE MIX 183

ROOTBEER, HOME BREWED 96

SMOOTHIE, BERRY SUMMER 171

TEA, SWEET 152

WATER, SUNSHINE 151

APPETIZERS, CONDIMENTS, AND SNACKS

APPLESAUCE, OLD FASHIONED. 29

BBQ SALT. 59

BBQ SAUCE, ROOTBEER 95

BUFFALO JERKY 69

BUTTER, PEAR 156

BUTTER, STRAWBERRY BLACK PEPPER 116

CANNING AND PRESERVING BASICS 158

CANNING FRUIT SYRUP 155

CHEERIOS NUGGETS 176

CHERRY PRESERVES, GROUND 50

CHIPS, COWBOY. 62

FRUITS AND VEGETABLES, HOME-DRIED . . . 157

HONEY, PEAR 44

LARD, RENDERED 56

MAYONNAISE, HOMEMADE 199

NACHOS, BUCKAROO. 104

POPCORN DELIGHT 126

RHUBARB SAUCE, YUMMY. 29

SALMON DIP 67

SALSA, CHERI'S SUPERB 85

SALSA, PEACH RASPBERRY 86

SALSA, ROJO (RED) 92

SALSA, VERDE (GREEN). 85

SAUERKRAUT, HOMEMADE 159

SAUSAGE ROUNDS, BBQ 56

TRAIL MIX, BAREBACK 23

This book is dedicated to our wonderful and irreplaceable children: Lori Anne, Heidi Marie, Cheri Kaye, Luke Lamar, Mark Anthony, Cameron Lee, and Heather Rose- faithful life traveling companions, along with your families.

And our little boy, Jude Cameron; our small son, age 3 ½ , who left us November 4th 1969, for a better land, we know he is in heaven waiting for us all.

We must mention our adopted boy that is still living with us, Jack Arden.

How do you thank your children for a lifetime of love? We have many warm memories of your childhood days! We hope you dear children can remember us with love and forgiveness as we know our imperfectness. May this book assist and support your teachings and through your examples may your children and grandchildren have the values of an honest life with food on your table and thanks to our Heavenly Father for all blessings.

With love and affection,
Mom and Dad

Our Father which art in heaven.
Hallowed be Thy name. Thy kingdom
come. Thy will be done in earth as it
is in heaven. Give us this day our daily
bread. And forgive us our trespasses, as we
forgive those who trespass against us.
And lead us not into temptation, but
deliver us from evil. For Thine is the
kingdom and the power and the glory,
forever and ever.

Amen.